TWAYNE'S WORLD AUTHORS SERIES

A Survey of the World's Literature

CHINA

William Schultz, University of Arizona

EDITOR

Li Ho

TWAS 537

李長吉

長吉將死時忽見一緋衣人駕赤虬持一版書若太古篆或霹靂石文者云當召長吉
長吉了不能讀欻下榻叩頭言阿婆老且病賀不願去阿婆長吉舉語時呼母云緋
衣人笑曰帝城白玉樓立召君為記天上差樂不苦也長吉獨涕邊人盡見之長吉氣
絕常所居窓中歘歘有煙氣聞行車嘒管之聲其母急止人哭待之如炊五斗黍許時長
吉竟死。

Li Ho

LI HO

By KUO-CH'ING TU

University of California, Santa Barbara

TWAYNE PUBLISHERS
A DIVISION OF G. K. HALL & CO., BOSTON

Library of Congress Cataloging in Publication Data

Tu, Kuo-ch'ing, 1941–
Li Ho.

(Twayne's world authors series ; TWAS 537 : China)
Bibliography: p. 154–60
Includes index.
1. Li, Ho, 790–816—Criticism and interpretation.
PL2677.L5Z88   895.1'1'3   78-31946
ISBN 0-8057-6379-1

For Lucian

Contents

About the Author

Kuo-ch'ing Tu, born in Taiwan, 1941, received his B.A. in English literature from National Taiwan University, M.A. in Japanese literature from Kwansei Gakuin University, Japan, and Ph.D. in Chinese literature from Stanford University. He is Assistant Professor of Eastern Languages and Literatures, University of California, Santa Barbara. He has written and published four books of his own poems and translated T. S. Eliot's *The Waste Land*, Charles Baudelaire's *Les Fleurs du Mal* and James J. Y. Liu's *The Art of Chinese Poetry* into Chinese.

Preface

The poet Li Ho (style, Ch'ang-chi, 790–816), .well-known for his obscure, sensuous, and elaborate images, has been dubbed a "ghostly, demonic genius" *(kuei-ts'ai)* for his untraditional treatment of fantastic and macabre themes. In this regard his position in the history of classical Chinese poetry is a unique one.

Although his unorthodox poems were not included in most standard anthologies, such as the eighteenth-century *Three Hundred T'ang Poems*, he has not been, as A. C. Graham claims in his *Poems of the Late T'ang*, "a poet recently rediscovered after long neglect." Fifteen years after Li Ho's death, Tu Mu (803–852) wrote a preface to his poetry and Li Shang-yin (812?–858) wrote a short biography of him; Li especially admired him and was much influenced by his works. Since the Sung period (960–1279), Li Ho's poetry has been annotated and commented on by at least twenty editors or critics. Many Sung scholars were fond of paying Li Ho the great honor of contrasting his ghostly or demonic genius *(kuei)* with the Taoist immortal genius *(hsien)* of Li Po (701–762). The fact that the eminent Ch'ing scholar and commentator Wang Ch'i (ca. eighteenth century) also commented on Li Ho further attests to his importance.

In the past forty years, Li Ho's complete works have been translated with annotations into Japanese by three Japanese scholars, including the famous sinologist Suzuki Torao (1878–1963). Japanese studies of Li Ho utilize three further approaches: (1) statistical, represented by Arai Ken and Kamio Ryūsuke, each of whom, on the basis of word count (their statistics differ), draws his own conclusions based on such considerations as the frequency of color words and the word "death" *(ssu)*; (2) biographical, represented by Kusamori Shin'ichi, whose energetic work *The Pinions-drooping Traveler*: *Biography of Li Ch'ang-chi (Suishi no kyaku: Ri Chōkichi den)* has been published serially since 1965 and, at sixty chapters in two parts, is apparently less than half complete; (3) historical research, represented by Harada Kenyū, who has published at least thirty articles inquiring into facts and personalities relevant to Li Ho's life and times, and interpreting Li Ho's poems on the basis of such studies. Recently he has devoted his efforts to a private journal, *Ri*

Ga Kenkyū (Li Ho Studies), fourteen issues of which have appeared since January, 1971.

The earliest English translation of a poem by Li Ho appeared in 1901 in Herbert A. Giles' *A History of Chinese Literature*. It was not until 1947 that the first English anthology containing examples of Li Ho's work was published. In that year nineteen of his poems were translated by Ho Chih-yüan and included in Robert Payne's *The White Pony*. Before these translations appeared, Li Ho was almost entirely unknown to Western readers. In 1965, A. C. Graham's *Poems of the Late T'ang* included twenty-two of his poems, giving him considerable prominence among later T'ang poets. Finally, *The Poems of Li Ho*, translated by J. D. Frodsham, appeared in 1970.

In addition to translations, there are several unpublished doctoral dissertations on Li Ho (see the appended bibliography). Either these are comparative or historical studies of the poet's life and times, or else they concentrate on one particular aspect of Li Ho's poetry, e.g., its poetic diction or its mythological themes. In fact, a comprehensive critical study of Li Ho, focusing on the works themselves, has not hitherto been undertaken in English.

The present work consists of four chapters. The first chapter deals with the development of Li Ho's poetic mind as observed through his works. The biographical and historical background given in this chapter suggests that for this poet of such delicate constitution life was a dreary dream through which he moved, his only support being the "sword" of his poetic genius.

The second and third chapters focus on the poetry of Li Ho. The approach is based on Professor James J. Y. Liu's conception of poetry as exploration of worlds and of language as expounded in his excellent book, *The Art of Chinese Poetry*.

Professor Liu defines a poetic "world" as a synthesis of aspects of both external and internal realities, which combine to make up a new reality composed not only of natural objects, scenes, events, and action but also of a poet's thoughts, memories, sensations, and fantasies. In other words, a "world" in poetry is at once a "reflection of the poet's external environment and an expression of his total consciousness." Furthermore, Professor Liu contends that the poem is not merely a dead *description* of past events but a vivid *exploration* of the living moment in which past experience merges with the immediate experience of writing. Poetry is seen as a double exploration: "to find adequate words for new worlds of experience and to find new words for old familiar worlds." Of this there are two dimensions: the *depth* to which the new "world" is explored and the *breadth* of the language used in forming it. Therefore, two major criteria are applied in my study of Li Ho's poetry: the extent to which the poet has explored new territory and the extent to which he has explored the use of language.

Based on these ideas, then, the second chapter deals with the worlds of Li Ho's poetry. It contains two parts: one inquiring into the gloomy side of the poet's mind, a world of personal frustration and sorrow which often leads into ghostly realms and supernatural fantasies; the other discussing worlds of aesthetic experience, historical events, and social realities which are observed with detachment or even a critical spirit. In some of these worlds, Li Ho appears to be the first explorer.

The third chapter treats Li Ho's language in order to discover how the poet breaks new ground in the use of language. This chapter discusses aspects of poetic language, such as diction, syntax, versification, and symbolism, as well as the musical qualities of euphony and rhythm. One of the most interesting characteristics of Li Ho's poetry is its sensuous imagery, especially synaesthesia. Other specific features in Li Ho's use of language are also discussed.

The fourth chapter is an evaluation. Li Ho's poetic qualities are summed up as "dark" *(yu)*, "bright" *(ming)*, "startling" *(ch'i)*, and "splendid" *(li)*, the former two concerning his worlds, the latter regarding his language. All four qualities derive from the nature of *kuei* which, in traditional usage, has a double meaning: as a noun referring to a departed spirit (now dark, now bright), and as an adjective describing unearthly or nonhuman exquisiteness (startling or splendid). Furthermore, the sources of these four poetic qualities are traced to the influences Li Ho received from his predecessors. As a "ghostly and demonic genius" *(kuei-ts'ai)*, Li Ho forms an interesting trio with Li Po, a "poet-immortal" *(shih-hsien)*, and Tu Fu (712–770), a "poet-sage" *(shih-sheng)*, representing three different poetic sensibilities in traditional Chinese literary history. The book concludes with a review of some appraisals of the poet by modern scholars.

In connection with the study of Li Ho's life, Li Ho's chronology is a problem worth noting. Tu Mu's preface to *Li Ch'ang-chi ko-shih (Li Ch'ang-chi's Songs and Poems)* provides the only source for tracing and estimating his dates. As Tu Mu indicates in his preface, it was in the middle of the tenth month of the fifth year of T'ai-ho (831) that Shen Tzu-ming, an intimate friend of Li Ho's, sent Tu Mu a letter asking him to write a preface to Li Ho's works. Further- more, as Tu Mu indicates, Li Ho had died fifteen years previously at the age of twenty-seven. Assuming that Tu Mu wrote the preface in the same year it was requested, Li Ho should have died fifteen years before 831, and should have been born twenty-seven years before that. However, later scholars have two different ways of counting back fifteen years from 831: one way is to include 831 as a full year and trace the date of Li Ho's death back to 817; the other is to exclude 831 and trace it back to 816, a difference of one year. As to the method of counting back to establish the birth year, all scholars agree with the traditional Chinese way of counting a fraction of a year as one full year, yet some arrive at the year 791 while others take it to be 790. As a result, two sets of dates have been used for Li Ho's birth and death: 790–816 and 791–817. Most Chinese scholars adopt the dates 790–816, while almost all Japanese and English scholars adopt the dates 791–817. I agree with the traditional Chinese opinion for the following reasons: although the Chinese consider a person's age to be one year at birth, this system probably does not apply to counting the years that have elapsed since a per- son's death. To say that someone who died in the last month of last year has already been dead for two years is probably equally ridicu- lous to Chinese and Westerners. In support of the dates 791–817, M. T. South argues that

Li Ho was a candidate for the *Chin-shih* examination of the fifth year of Yüan-ho (810). His own words [in poems written at the time] suggest that this took place when he was twenty years old. Since, according to the old tradition, every Chinese person became one year older at the New Year, one can assume that at the beginning of the fifth year of Yüan-ho, Li Ho entered his twentieth year, and therefore, that the year of his birth must have been the seventh year of Chen-yüan (791) and the year of his death the twelfth year of Yüan-ho (817). [*Li Ho: A Scholar-official of the Yüan-ho Period*, pp. 117–118]

However, to take a number in a poetic line so literally, especially a line written under the requirements of poetic meter, can be hazard- ous and questionable. First of all, the bisyllabic word for "twenty" (*erh-shih*) fits rhythmically into the line concerned (*wo tang erh- shih pu te yi* or *erh-shih hsin yi hsiu*), and Li Ho could very well be using poetic license to fulfill the metric requirements of the line. Twenty-one *(erh-shih-yi)* would have added another syllable and would not fit into the rhythmic pattern. If we follow the 790–816 dates, Li Ho would actually have been twenty-one at the time, but there is really nothing to prevent him from giving his age as twenty, a round figure, especially when it fulfills an immediate poetic need.

In support of the 790 date, it is worth noting that Li Ho might have been born in the year of the *Horse*, because he wrote at least twenty-three poems on horses which appear to express metaphorically his own ambitions, expectations, and frustrations. The eleventh year of Chen-yüan (790) happened to be the year of the *Horse*. This was pointed out by Professor Yeh Ch'ing-ping in 1969, though his suggestion seems not to have attracted the attention of Japanese or English-speaking scholars.

The present volume is the synthesis of my prior studies of the works of Li Ho and I owe much to the insights of previous scholars, but at the same time I would like to think that I may have contributed some valid interpretations of my own. This study is intended as an introduction to these poems for the general reader and an extensive bibliography in primary sources and in English is provided for those interested in further pursuing the subject of Li Ho's life and works. For myself, this book is only the beginning of more intensive study and original research in the future.

I owe much to the many people who supported and assisted me in bringing this volume to publication. In particular, I owe a special debt of gratitude to Professor James J. Y. Liu of Stanford University under whose supervision the original work was undertaken which lead to my dissertation and finally to this book, and special thanks to the following people: To my friends Timothy Wong and Stuart Sargent for reading my original manuscript. To Messieurs Chao T'ien-yi and Suzuki Masao for expediting the availability of materials related to Li Ho in Chinese and Japanese. To my colleague in the Department of Eastern Languages, University of California at Santa Barbara, Professor Chauncey S. Goodrich and to Dr. Dorris Goodrich, for reading the original manuscript of this volume in detail and providing many valuable suggestions. To Dr. Patia Isaku for her assistance in improving my translations and for giving me the benefit of her broad knowledge of Western literature. To Patricia Woelk, my research assistant, for her invaluable help in organizing and revising the manuscript and for her fresh insights into some of

Li Ho's lines. To Mr. Henry Tai, Supervisor of the Oriental Collection, UCSB Library, for his special efforts in acquiring materials for my study, and Mr. Peter Pang of the UCSB Oriental Collection for regularly apprising me of new information relevant to my research. To Mr. Yin Chuang at Stanford University for providing materials from Hoover Library. To Professor William Schultz of the University of Arizona, editor of the China section of the Twayne World Author Series, for his kind assistance and advice. And, of course, to my wife Seiko for her patience during my long hours of study and for her help in typing this manuscript.

This book would not have been possible without the support of a grant from the University of California Regents' Humanities Fellowship Committee which made possible my trip to Japan and Taiwan to further this research, and a general research grant from UCSB to help with the final revision.

K. C. T.

Acknowledgments

I wish to express my gratitude and acknowledgment to Berkeley Research Publishing Service for permission to reprint material from my article in *Essays in Chinese Poetry*, Volume I, © 1978, James Miller, ed., and to The University of Chicago Press for material from James J. Y. Liu, *The Art of Chinese Poetry*, © 1962 by James J. Y. Liu.

Chronology

790 Born in Ch'ang-ku of Fu-ch'ang county *(hsien)* in modern Honan province.

796 Earliest literary composition (according to legend).

804 Well known for his songs and poems in ballad style *(yüeh-fu)*.

806 Hair at his temples already gray.

807 Travelled to Loyang to visit Han Yü and impressed him with his songs and poems. His father died (?).

809 In Loyang, Han Yü and Huang-fu Shih visited him.

810 In autumn, took the district examination in Honan-*fu* and received a grade of "outstanding" *(chün)*. In winter, went to Ch'ang-an to take the *chü* examination for the *chin-shih* degree. Was prevented from taking the examination.

811 In late autumn, returned to Ch'ang-ku.

812 In spring, given a post as Supervisor of Ceremonies in Ch'ang-an.

813 In spring, resigned from office and returned in poor health to Ch'ang-ku to recuperate.
In autumn, left Ch'ang-ku for Ch'ang-an again.

814 In autumn, went to Lu-chou, in modern Shansi province, to ask help of Chang Ch'e.

815 In winter, in Chang Ch'e's house, health gave out.

816 In winter, returned to Ch'ang-ku and died.

CHAPTER 1

The Weary Dream of a Delicate Swordsman: A Biographical Sketch

LI Ho, styled Ch'ang-chi, a native of Ch'ang-ku in Fu-ch'ang county, Honan, was born in A.D. 790. His father, Chin-su, supposedly the poet Tu Fu's twenty-ninth younger cousin, took service on the border and was at one time the magistrate of Shan county. His mother was from the Cheng family; he had an older sister and a younger brother.

Born to a family in reduced circumstances and descended from the imperial house of T'ang, Li Ho's whole life was dominated by the tension between two opposing factors: relative poverty and the pride of imperial ancestry.

Whether by nature or because of his poverty, Li Ho had a delicate constitution and suffered much from poor health. It is said of his appearance that he was thin, with bushy eyebrows and long finger-nails, and that before he had even reached eighteen, the hair at his temples had turned white.[1]

In many poems Li Ho refers to himself as "imperial descendant" or "scion of the Princes of T'ang." His biographies in both the *Old T'ang History* and the *New T'ang History* also say that he was descended from a Prince of Cheng of the T'ang royal family.[2] Nevertheless, in the "Genealogical Tables of the Royal House" in the *New T'ang History*, the names of both Li Ho and his father are missing. Be that as it may, Li Ho's consciousness of imperial ancestry was extremely strong. Despite his poverty, he was very proud of his uncommon origin:

> This horse is no common horse;
> It is the very spirit of the Equine Stars.
> Come forward, rap on its thin bones,
> They still carry the sound of bronze.[3]

At the age of seven, Li Ho was already able to create literary compositions. According to one anecdote,

When the eminent scholar Han Yü [768–824] and the literary master Huang-fu Shih [ca. 777–?] saw what Li Ho had written, they marvelled, but had not yet met the man. They said to each other: "If he is a man of the past, he is someone we do not know; if he is a man of today, how could we not have heard of him?" Someone chanced to inform them that the writer was the son of Chin-su, whereupon both went on horseback to visit him and asked to see his son. When Ho came out to greet them, his hair in tufts and wearing boy's clothes, they were hardly able to believe this was the author they had come to meet. They then asked him to write some poems. Ho happily took up a writing tablet and dipped his brush as if no one was there beside him. He wrote a poem entitled "The Imposing Official Carriage Passes for a Visit" . . . The two masters were greatly astonished.[4]

Although this kind of child-prodigy tale is almost an obligatory convention in anecdotes of the lives of Chinese literary figures, it may be assumed that Li Ho did have some precocious talent. In another anecdote, Li Ho is again said to have astonished Han Yü, having appeared uninvited at his door, bringing with him some songs and poems of his own composition:

At that time, Han Yü held the post of Professor at the Loyang branch of the University of Sons of State. He had just seen guests to the door and was extremely exhausted when his gatekeeper presented him with Ho's manuscripts. While loosening his sash, he glanced over them, his eye coming to rest on two lines from the first poem, "Ballad of the Grand Warden of Yen Gate":

> Black clouds press upon the city wall;
>   the city wall is about to be crushed.
> Armor-shine toward the moon, golden scales
>   open.

Having read these, Han Yü immediately fastened his sash again and gave orders to call Ho in.[5]

Both these anecdotes depict the tremendous impact of Li Ho's poetic imagery upon his readers. His poetic genius was such that by the age of fifteen he was already well known, especially for his *yüeh-fu*[6] songs and poems in the ballad style.

In addition to the pressures of poverty and his personal drive to live with a dignity befitting one of imperial blood, self-confidence in his own literary abilities may well have motivated Li Ho to take the examination for the *chin-shih* degree, the first step toward a high-ranking official career.[7]

In the autumn of 810, Li Ho, as a youth of twenty-one, went to take the district examination in Honan. He received a grade of "outstanding" *(chün)*. Next he went to the capital at Ch'ang-an to take the *chü* examination for the *chin-shih* degree. As a rule, a district candidate had to be presented by a government official who would also act as his political patron in his future governmental career. In Li Ho's case, he was recommended by Han Yü, magistrate of Honan, and Huang-fu Shih, censor in the Court of General Affairs, both of whom, according to the anecdotes above, had been so greatly impressed by Li Ho's poetic talent.

Armed with a great poetic gift and weighty recommendations, Li Ho was filled with confidence and hope. In the winter of 810, he spurred his horse and dashed off to Ch'ang-an:

> I have a sword that bids adieu to my homeland,
> Its jade edge can cut the clouds.
> A champion gallops his horse to Hsiang-yang,[8]
> His very spirit bearing the Spring.
> At dawn I resent my sword's unspotted gleam;
> At dusk I resent my sword's cold glare.
> I can hold my sword toward other men,
> Not knowing how to hold it to reflect my own body.[9]
>
> [p. 40]

Li Ho's sword, his brilliant poetic mind, was anxious to try its luck. However, when he arrived at Ch'ang-an after dashing the entire two hundred and fifty miles from his home, he was dazed by the discovery that a strange rumor about him had been spread throughout the capital. Having displayed at age seven a talent for writing, and having earned a reputation as a poet in the capital by the age of fifteen, and, moreover, being recommended by the illustrious scholar-officials Han Yü and Huang-fu Shih, Li Ho had become so well known and his success in the examination had appeared so assured that someone had been inspired to slander him. One of his competitors in the *chin-shih* examination had raised the point that "As Ho's father's name is Chin-su, Ho should not sit for

the *chin-shih* examination." In the event of a successful completion
of the examination, Li Ho's assumption of the *chin-shih* title would
have violated a taboo. The *chin* in the title is a homophone of the
Chin in Li Ho's father's name; customary law required that one
avoid either in speech or in writing the name of one's father.[10] Yet
this appears to have been only a pretext used to deny Li Ho the
opportunity of sitting for the examination. The real reason may lie in
Li Ho's own character; his own insufferable arrogance may have
alienated many of those around him and led to his downfall.

One account attributes the rumor to another poet, Yüan Chen
(779–831), who admired Ho and went to visit him. Ho, however,
turned him away with a disparaging remark.[11] In another account,

The Vice-Chancellor Li Fan [754–811] was compiling a collection of Li Ho's
songs and poems and wanted to furnish it with a preface. Hearing of a
cousin and former classmate of Ho's, Li Fan called him in and asked him to
search for omissions. The cousin thanked Li for his interest and said, "I have
obtained all of Ho's original manuscripts. If you let me see all of your
collections, I would gladly revise them." Lord Li was pleased and gave him
all he had. After a whole year, with no word from the cousin, Lord Li
became angry, called him in again and demanded an explanation. The man
replied, "Ho and I have lived together since childhood; I hate his haughty
attitude and have been thinking of how to pay him back. I took the poems I
received from you, along with those I had myself, and tossed them all down
the privy." Lord Li was furious, rebuked the man and drove him out. He
sighed for a long time. For this reason, few of Ho's works were handed
down.[12]

Had there been anyone among those competing with Li Ho in the
examination who had been insulted or slighted by him, like his
cousin or Yüan Chen, the rumor could have arisen from these quarters. At the same time, however, the arrow of slander seems to have
been directed not only at Li Ho but also at those who encouraged
him to take the examination. As Huang-fu Shih said to Han Yü, "If
you don't clear up this affair, both you and Ho will get into trouble."[13] Thus the rumor may have originated not from among the
competing candidates, but from among the candidates' rival pa-
trons. Chinese tradition has it that a literary man is a statesman and
vice versa; therefore, Han Yü's sponsorship of Li Ho or any other
promising juniors may have been both to create a literary school of
his own and to establish political influence. Li Ho may have been an

innocent victim of a political struggle among the candidates' sponsors.[14]

At any rate, it is worthy of note that while no extant poems written by Li Ho after this incident refer to Han Yü, there are four poems referring to Huang-fu Shih. In one, entitled "In the Jen-ho Quarter: a Desultory Talk with Huang-fu Shih," Li Ho recalls the disaster at Ch'ang-an and expresses his appreciation of Huang-fu Shih's sponsorship:

> In vain was I honored to be called Friend;
>   I have offended in your sight.
> Just as you began to pull me up, the strong
>   rope snapped.
> Escorted by the Loyang wind, the horse entered
>   the far-off passes;
> The palace gates yet unopened, it fell among mad dogs.
>
> [p. 58]

Li Ho, unexpectedly assaulted by "mad dogs," was deprived of the right to take the *chin-shih* examination. In front of the office of the Ministry of Rites, a crowd of people jostled one another for a look at the list announcing the successful candidates. Among the twenty *chin-shih* produced in 811, Li Ho's name was of course not listed. All alone he hid at an inn in a corner of the capital and, "Lonely on a stranger's pillow, watched the Spring grow old" (p. 58).

Li Ho remained at Ch'ang-an for some time. Knowing that his old mother and younger brother both eagerly awaited the news of his certain success, he muttered to himself: "My family has entertained great expectations, In hopes I will fill their hungry bellies" (p. 137).

Imagining himself to be a knight on horseback bearing the spirit of Spring to Ch'ang-an, how could he have known that he would be ruined by his father's name? Certainly he felt great bitterness and disillusionment:

> When I was twenty, I did not gain the day;
> My whole heart grieves, withers like a blighted orchid.
>
> [p. 92]

> In Ch'ang-an there was a young man,
> At twenty his heart already decayed.
>
> [p. 84]

Li Ho stayed until it seemed certain that he could never take the *chin-shih* examination. Lonely and disappointed, he left Ch'ang-an in the late autumn of 811.

> Snow falls, cassia blossoms scarce,
> A crying crow, struck by a shot, returns.
> In the water by the pass, a donkey rider's reflection,
> In the winds of Ch'in, my hat slouches, tassel dangling.
> Returning home is a trial of ten thousand miles;
> Carrying back no official seal is of itself lamentable.
> My beloved hesitates to ask me,[15]
> In the mirror, her image with two streams of tears.
>
> [pp. 76–77]

From Ch'ang-an to Ch'ang-ku, Li Ho's home, is only a distance of three hundred miles, but

> He returned, his bones thin, no color in his face,
> Disease rushing to his head, his sidelocks sparse.
>
> [pp. 58–59]

To him those three hundred miles were an endless trial.

* * *

Devastated by the slander and its tragic consequences, Li Ho returned to the pastoral beauty of his home in Ch'ang-ku to recuperate. His house was surrounded by gardens planted with bamboos, mulberries, melons, flowers, and bushes. Planting melons or water chestnuts, roaming through the bamboo gardens, he tried to divert his thoughts.

> I scrape off its green luster to inscribe the *Songs of
>   the South*;[16]
> Rich fragrance, vernal powder, line on line in black.
> Be they without feeling or full of sorrow, who will see?
> Dew-burdened, mist-tearful, innumerable branches.
>
> [p. 64]

Sometimes it seems he wished only to lose himself in nature:

> Having no heart to tailor songs, I lie down in
>   the Spring breeze
>
> [p. 43]

> Aged, I will go to the head of the stream to become
> an old angler.
>
> [p. 43]

Still, the spirit of the "champion galloping his horse to Hsiang-yang" had not completely died away. It smoldered in his heart and could vent itself only in poems he believed no one would hear. He lamented:

> Searching for the sentence, choosing the phrase,
> I grow old, carving insects.[17]
>
> [p. 42]

> What place is there for writings to wail in the
> Autumn wind?
>
> [p. 42]

He scolded himself:

> Why did this young man not wear a sword,
> Recover the passes and mountains of fifty counties?[18]
>
> [p. 42]

He exclaimed:

> Now I will buy a Jo-jeh River sword;[19]
> Tomorrow morning I will go to serve and learn
> from Lord Monkey.[20]
>
> [p. 42]

At first glance it appears that Li Ho's spirit had revived. In spite of his delicate healt' he dreamed of being a swordsman, if only symbolically. In fact, his wishful ranting can only be taken as a kind of psychological compensation for his frustrated ambition. In the opinion of Kusamori Shin'ichi, the Japanese author of Li Ho's biography, "Li Ho's unyielding spirit of heroism was a disguise, an exposure of weakness, the bluster of a weakling, the energetic fantasy of a sick, raw youth. It was a dream of revenge in his fantasy which, fanned by his humiliation, had become still more confused."[21] Lu Hsün (1881–1936), the modern Chinese writer, also disbelieved Li Ho's high-flown words of being a swordsman. "The long-nailed, skinny-like-a-stick Li Ho simply overestimates his own ability; a hundred percent discount should be given to his words, because he actually did not go off to become a swordsman."[22]

Nevertheless, Li Ho's dream of being a swordsman was not completely whimsical. Since the rebellion of An Lu-shan (755–763), the provincial military governors in northern China had become more and more recalcitrant.[23] Skilled warriors could find ready employment either on their staffs or as loyal defenders of the emperor's position. Li Ho seems to have believed that at such a time if he had thrown down the pen and taken up the sword, he could have had a different future.

Thus Li Ho's spirit resembled a sword. When his sickness worsened and his fever heightened, the sword became molten; with the passing of the fever, his sword began to glitter, weaving a dream of revenge.

Lo Ho's mind resembled an improperly balanced scale, always wavering up and down between his ambition and his sick body, between Ch'ang-an and Ch'ang-ku. When he fell seriously ill, his mind leaned to his native home; at home his mind inclined to Ch'ang-an as soon as he became better.

In the spring of 812, Li Ho was given a post as Supervisor of Ceremonies in Ch'ang-an, probably by virtue of his ancestors' services.

His duties were very simple and dull in spite of the high-sounding title. He had to see to it that the ceremonial vessels were set out properly in the imperial ancestral temple, attend to seating arrangements at court audiences, and give signals to bow, kneel, kowtow, or rise during ceremonies. Li Ho had good reasons to be dissatisfied with this position:

> In wind and snow I served at the Altar of Fasting,
> My black ribbon piercing my bronze seal.
> Manner and bearing, a cross between a slave and a maidservant
> Whose sole wish is to take over the dustpans and brooms.
> When will the eye of Heaven open,
> And an old sword have a chance to utter a roar?
>
> [pp. 84–85]

Li Ho's sword, with its jade edge that could cut the clouds, never having been called to service, had become a broom, with which "Having swept away the last horse's hoof-print,/Back from the office, I shut the gate myself"[24] (p. 20).

Like General Lü[25] who, valiant as he was, had no chance to go to
the front and could only weep at the emperor's tomb:

> In the north, rebellious air soils the blue sky;
> The dragon-sword cries at night while the General
>   is left to idle.
>
> [p. 129]

Nevertheless, in Ch'ang-an Li Ho was sometimes invited to go on
outings with princes and their courtesans, or to join parties given by
young nobles and friends. When he was in a state of drunken
ecstasy, his face glowing, he recollected his frustrated past.

> Things on my mind are like great waves;
> I sit in their midst, startled, time and time again.
>
> [p. 53]

Sometimes he was asked by those noble princes to write songs for
the girls to play and sing. He deemed it an honor; his pride was
somehow gratified.

> On Hsiang-ju's tomb, autumn cypresses have grown;[26]
> Today in the capital who is the troubadour who sings
>   of love?
> With piled-up hair and drunken eyes, the girl beseeches
>   the noble lords:
> "Pay my respects to the Imperial Scion, this Ts'ao Chih!"[27]
>
> [pp. 135–136]

But sometimes he felt his pride was hurt, and he burned with a kind
of jealousy:

> To request a song, go ahead and request the songs of
>   nobles and ministers.
> The Supervisor of Ceremonies is a low official, what
>   could his songs be worth?
>
> [p. 155]

When depressed, Li Ho often expressed his feelings of self-
abhorrence by describing himself as physically ugly. The more depressed he got and the more he suffered, the more ugly and shabby
he became in his poems. He held the post of Supervisor of Cere-

monies for only about three years, but it was a time of continual depression; he pictured himself "Haggard and worn like a straw dog"[28] (p. 84).

This "ugly" Li Ho can also be discerned in his poems on the horse:

> Starving, prostrate, with hawthorne-twig bones,
> Coarse hair pricking out broken flowers;[29]
> Mane scorched, vermilion hue fallen,
> Forelocks cut, lacerated by a long hemp rope.
>
> [p. 47]

Or

> Shu of Liao died suddenly, imperceptibly,[30]
> And now no one rears dragons.
> Night comes, frost overwhelms the stable,
> The thoroughbred's bones break in the west wind.
>
> [p. 48]

In a further involution of feelings, it appears that the more he thought of himself as ugly, the more frequent was his dream of the sword:

> In gloom I sleep, my pillow a sword-case.
> Under the inn's bedcurtains, I dream I'm created a peer.
>
> [p. 83]

However, when he awoke and wandered about the capital, his "ugliness" crept up on him again, attacked him, scoffed at him, until he cried out madly

> Clothes tattered like flying quail-feathers,
>   my horse like a dog,
> Facing the crossroads, I beat my sword to raise
>   a bronze-throated roar!
>
> [p. 92]

It was a roar echoing the bronze sound of the uncommon horse's thin bones, coming from the nadir of his fortune, a roar of agony and anger. Seeing with his own eyes

> Ch'ang-an, a kingdom of jade and cassia,
> Halberds' pennants cover noble gates,
>
> [p. 138]

Li Ho felt ashamed of himself,

> A petty man like dead ashes,
> Heart cut, sprouting autumn thorns.
>
> [p. 138]

In fact, Ch'ang-an was too expensive for him. In his straitened circumstances, the unbalanced scale of his mind began to incline toward his native home:

> Under the tavern sign I got off my horse,
> taking off my autumn clothes.
> I pawned them and bought a pot of Yi-yang wine.
>
> [p. 92]

Only the wine of Yi-yang, another name for Ch'ang-ku, Li Ho's native place, could banish his sorrow and illness, and even then only temporarily.

In the spring of 813, Li Ho resigned from office and reluctantly left Ch'ang-an.[31]

> Grass warm, clouds dizzy, ten thousand miles
> of Spring,
> Palace flowers stroke my face, seeing off the
> wayfarer.
> I say to myself: the sword of Han should
> fly far,[32]
> Why is this homebound carriage burdened
> with my sick body?
>
> [p. 19]

Another defeat.

* * *

Li Ho returned to Ch'ang-ku again. Only the mountains and waters of home could cure and solace his sick body and frustrated spirit. As Li Shang-yin tells us in his biography of Li Ho,

From time to time Li Ho left his house mounted on a donkey, followed by a page boy with an old ragged brocade bag on his back. When occasionally inspired, he would scribble a line and drop it in the bag. At nightfall when he returned home, his mother would have her maid receive the bag and empty it out. When she saw that he had written so much, she always used to say: "My son will not stop until he has vomited up his heart." She would then light the lamp and give him his meal. Li Ho would take from the maidservant what he had written, grind some ink, fold some paper, complete the poems, and put them into another bag. Unless he was very drunk or it was a day of offering condolences at a funeral, it was usually like this.[33]

Writing poetry had become Li Ho's daily work. He had suffered too much; he had so much to write. He could not stop writing even if he should really vomit out his heart.

Li Ho was very grateful to the page boy who followed him every day either up mountains or down into the valley of Ch'ang-ku. Li Ho wrote a poem for him entitled "While Studying in Ch'ang-ku I Showed this Poem to my Page Boy from Pa:"

> Insects sing, the lamplight dims;
> The night is cold, the fumes of medicine heavy.
> You pity me, a champion with drooping wings;
> Hard though it is, you still follow me.
>
> [p. 76]

Li Ho also wrote the boy's reply:

> A big nose goes well with mountain clothing;
> Bushy-browed, you enter into painstaking chant.
> If it were not you who sang *yüeh-fu* songs,[34]
> Who would understand the depth of sorrowful Autumn?
>
> [p. 76]

Late on an autumn night, perhaps Li Ho's mother, younger brother and maidservant were all asleep. Under the starry sky, only the chirping of insects was to be heard. Li Ho sat in a dimly lit room, his bushy eyebrows knitted, composing his sorrowful poems. His young servant, beside him, squatted in front of a kettle, watching the fumes of medicine rise.

Thus Li Ho recuperated at home. From his failures in Ch'ang-an he had acquired some wisdom and a better understanding of himself:

> I realize I am no tiger breaking out of a cage;
> I am content to be a panther hiding in the mist.
>
> [p. 99]

> This fretful man of Ch'eng-chi[35]
> Would do well to learn from Chih-yi Tzu-p'i.[36]
>
> [p. 102]

However, Li Ho's worldly ambitions never died. When his health improved, he began to dream again.

> One who replied to royal verse in the palace,
> Under an autumn quilt, dreams of bronze carriages.
>
> [p. 18]

> The king of Ch'in cannot be seen;[37]
> Dawn to dusk therein grows my internal fever.
>
> [p. 62]

In the autumn of 813, the panther veiled in mist became a tiger breaking out of the cage. Li Ho left Ch'ang-ku again.

> I've rolled up the mats on my eastern bed.
> Forlorn and helpless, I'm going on another
>   journey.
> The autumn white in the far, far void,
> The sun fills the road before my gates.
>
> [p. 77]

This time, however, it seems Li Ho had no definite destination. The road ahead was as bright as the autumn wilds and as white as the autumn wind. It seems he was driven to leave home by his desire for self-respect as a man. He realized that "Already born, I have to feed myself" (p. 69), so "with a burden on my back, I went out of my gate" (p. 69). Once out of his gate, though, he asked himself, "But where to?"

At the end of the tenth month, in spite of snow and sleet, cold and dark, he kept pushing on until he arrived at the rear gate of Loyang. But Loyang was not his journey's end. He began to hesitate. "At first I wanted to go south to Ch'u,/But then again, I would travel west to Ch'in" (p. 103).

He could not decide; therefore he went to visit a famous fortune-teller:

Please find out for me their intentions at the Palace.
How could they make of me a hewer of wood?

[p. 104]

His mind was made up to go west to try his fortune in Ch'ang-an,
the capital, situated in the area formerly belonging to the state of
Ch'in. It seems that no tangible result was attained on this journey;
no poems are left either.

In the autumn of 814, Li Ho went to Lu-chou in Shansi in hopes
that his friend Chang Ch'e (d. 822), who at that time was serving
there as an adviser, might be able to help him. However, it seems
that nothing but more disappointment resulted from this trip.

I, Ch'ang-chi of Lung-hsi, a ruined knight,[38]
With the last round of wine feel cramped to the core.
Linen clothes torn to pieces, Chao-ch'eng
    in autumn:[39]
I have chanted poems all night; the east
    whitens.

[p. 57]

In the winter of 815, in Chang Ch'e's house Li Ho's health gave
out.

Traveller's wine attacks my sorrow-stricken lungs;
Parting-songs linger round languid strings.
A poem seals two ribbons of tears;
The dew breaks a spray of orchid.

[pp. 79–80]

It seems that Li Ho was writing not just another poem but his own
elegy. In the winter of 816, he returned to Ch'ang-ku. The delicate
orchid that had begun to wither at twenty at last gave way under the
burden of dew.

In his biography of Li Ho, Li Shang-yin tells us:

When Li Ho was at the point of death, suddenly in daytime, he saw a man
in a dark red robe, riding a red dragon and carrying a tablet with characters
on it like ancient seal scripts or "thunderclap" inscriptions. He said: "I have
come to summon Li Ho." Ho could not read the inscriptions. He immediately got out of his bed, bowed and said: "Mommy is old and ill, I
cannot leave her." The man in the dark red robe said with a smile: "The

Emperor of Heaven has just completed the White Jade Tower and is summoning you to write a description of it. To live in Heaven is enjoyable, not bitter." Ho just wept. All those attending him saw it. In a little while, Ho gave up his breath. From the window where he used to sit, a mist rose into the air. The sounds of pipes and carriages were heard. His mother hastily kept everyone from weeping. After a while, about the time it takes to cook five pecks of millet, Ho finally died.[40]

Thus Li Ho died.[41] His weary dream of being a swordsman came to an end, as he himself had unwittingly prophesied:

> I say to myself: the sword of Han should
> fly far,
> Why is this homebound carriage burdened
> with my sick body?

[p. 19]

Li Ho's sword, his radiant, trenchant poetic spirit, finally soared into the sky, vanished like a wisp of cloud, leaving his sick body on the earth.

CHAPTER 2

Light and Shadows: His Worlds

I A Cold Emerald Candle Flickering at Night

POETRY is that expression of a poet's mind which, due to his innate disposition and experiences in life, exhibits particular inclinations and a characteristic sensibility. Li Ho had a naturally poor constitution; his life was a constant conflict between his pride in being a royal descendant and his bitterness at defeat in gaining an official position. His worlds are the reflections and expressions of a mind that had been shaped and sharpened by his sufferings and personal experiences.

Although it is hazardous to assume that we understand the poet's attitude when he wrote his poems, for the convenience of discussion Li Ho's poems can be divided into two basic groups: those written by the poet as a sufferer and those written as an observer. The former tend to be concerned with the poet's personal feelings, his sorrow, resentment, love, and hate; the latter deal mainly with the poet's circumstances, his observations and reflections on life, history, and society in general. This distinction is by no means clear-cut and absolute; a poetic mind usually does not work so simply. A "personal poem," in fact, often involves objectifying inner feelings, whereas an observation of the "objective world" must still be from some point of view, usually a personal one.

It seems to me that, while Li Ho was a poet with a tragic life, the morbid, gloomy, and pathetic aspects of his poetry have often been overemphasized. "Li Ho, who wrote more about light than anybody else," claims Kamio Ryūsuke, "was in fact more afraid of light than anybody else, and it was only in the darkness of night that his poetic interest was awakened. Essentially he was a poet of the night."[1] Or, as Seto Yasuo states, "In Li Ho's case, behind his pessimism lay the consciousness of his being an injured person. . . . therefore the

34

world reflected in Li Ho's mind, which nursed delusions of being injured, was truly 'an inferno'."[2] Although these observations are valid, there appears to be a conspicuous tendency, at least among Japanese scholars, to overemphasize Li Ho's suffering at the cost of overlooking his role as a profound observer of and commentator on the ambiguity of despair.[3] After moving beyond obvious levels, one is able to discern in this poetry a complexity and ingenuity that transcends personal suffering.

To examine the kinds of worlds Li Ho explored in his poetry one must first read the poems, analyze them, and finally discuss the individual poems. Since content and expression are so closely allied in Li Ho's poetry in particular, it is necessary to discuss the poems and the worlds within them as a whole. We begin with a typical example of those poems apparently motivated by or substantially concerned with his sufferings:

Song: A Grieved Heart

A choked voice imitating the songs of Ch'u,
Sick bones grieving in solitude's bleakness.
Autumnal figure, hair turning white,
A tree whose leaves wail in wind and rain.
Lamp blue-green, orchid-oil exhausted,
Around the fading glow, a flying moth dances.
An ancient wall covered with hardened dust,
The traveler's soul murmurs in dreams.

[p. 54]

I take this poem to be a portrayal of Li Ho's own life when he was immersed in the depths of despair and sickness. He echoes the sorrowful songs of Ch'u, most of which are attributed to the statesman and poet Ch'ü Yüan (343?–277? B.C.), a tragic figure with whom Li Ho often compares himself. While the first line expresses his spiritual sadness, the second line suggests his grief through a physiological correlative: his sick bones grieving in solitude's bleakness. *Yu-su* (solitude's bleakness) expresses his loneliness in autumn, traditionally regarded as a time of white bleakness (*su*) with concomitant implications of decay, grief, and despair. The next two lines develop further the poet's grief via a double image of himself as a body in decay and as a tree with wailing leaves. Since the poet also refers to his physical self as an "autumnal figure," these two lines constitute an image of three dimensions: a transitory autumn, a haggard man with white hair falling, and a withered tree shedding its leaves. Wind and rain, in many of Li Ho's poems, stand for time or natural forces that hasten people into decrepitude. The next two lines show the other, or the inners side, of the grieving heart. A lamplight turns bluish-green because it has burned up its energy, the orchid oil. The word "orchid" *(lan)* calls to mind Li Ho's line:

> My whole heart grieves, withers like a
> blighted orchid.

[p. 92]

"Orchid" symbolizes the poet's mind, an association stemming from Ch'ü Yüan's similar usage in the *Li Sao*.[4] Thus, this line suggests that the poet shares the same fate with the lamplight that sputters in its struggle to survive. In utter despair, the poet sees his fate in terms of the traditional metaphor of a flying moth pursuing a fading glow *(lo-chao):* either a dying light or the setting sun, but its use here is to indicate the dying lamplight; hence this poetic world at once includes the enclosed atmosphere of a room with a single dying lamp flame at night as well as the broad expanse of the outside world of a traveler facing the setting sun. The red fading glow in the western sky, resembling the dying lamplight, proclaims the end of day, and the traveler still wanders about like the fluttering moth approaching an inescapable and complete darkness. A sense of gloomy foreboding looms over the poet's mind. As the wall is covered with the hardened dust of the world, so is his mind shrouded with worldly cares. Buffeted by the world, his weary soul murmurs even in dreams: the journey of life seems to be just too long for him. The idea that life is like a journey is an old one, but here the metaphor expresses a subtle and highly original quality.

Thus this poem, as the title suggests, is a confession of the poet's grief; the world it unfolds is extremely lonely and desperate. However, even in such a personal poem as this the poet objectifies his own emotions, observing himself from a distance, succeeding in an escape from his own personality. The secret of writing an impersonal poem on personal suffering consists, as Li Ho shows in this poem, in the use of metaphors, especially images that substitute for the self. For example, instead of the personal pronoun "I", Li Ho refers to himself as the "sick bones," the "autumn figure," the "traveler's soul," etc. In avoiding personal pronouns, the poet expresses grief without limiting it to his own particular experience. This corresponds to T. S. Eliot's idea of "impersonality" in poetry: a "significant emotion" is achieved by means of the so-called "objective correlatives," a set of objects, a situation, a chain of events.[5] This is a prevalent usage in Chinese poetry in general, not particularly Li Ho's.

In the image of the moth pursuing a fading glow Li Ho sees a fate similar to his own. This sense of futility and sadness deriving from disappointment can also be perceived in the following poem:

Long Songs Follow Short Songs[6]

Long songs burst through my coat flap;
Short songs cut off my white hair.
The King of Ch'in cannot be seen;[7]
Dawn to dusk therein grows my internal fever.
Thirsty, I drink wine from the jug.
Hungry, I pull up millet on the dike.
Chilly, forlorn, the fourth month wanes,
A thousand miles at once turn green.

Mountain-tops at night—how endless;
The bright moon has fallen below the rocks.
As I roam along the rocks searching,
Its glow emerges beyond the high peaks.
I cannot play with the moon;
Before my song is done, the hair at my temples
  has turned.

[p. 62]

In this poem Li Ho uses hyperbole to express his disappointment—his long songs would "burst through his coat-flap" and his short songs would "cause his hair to fall out." In lonely despair, he notices that the earth has suddenly turned green, seemingly in mocking contrast to the forlornness of his heart. Thus Li Ho conjures up a contrast startlingly similar to that of the opening line of T. S. Eliot's *The Waste Land:* "April is the cruelest month."

In the second half of the poem, the poet gives dramatic expression to the reasons behind his forlornness. The bright moon offers the light he desires while the range of peaks in the night prevent the poet, in the depths of a valley, and implicitly in the depths of despair, from seeing the moon. However, rediscovering moonlight, the poet is so enraptured that he wanders along the boulders trying to approach it. But the poet then realizes that the moon will pass its zenith to disappear again, leaving him once more in darkness. In the gloom, he raises his head and sees its glowing orb beyond the high peaks, moving farther and farther away from him. In a Confucian interpretation, the distance is the alienation felt by the poet in his official life. The moon in this case stands for the emperor and the giant mountain peaks obscuring it from view are the flattering courtiers who surround the throne and prevent Li Ho from drawing closer.

The following poem expresses further apprehensions haunting the poet's mind:

Vast Song

The south wind blows away mountains to make
     level lands;
God sends T'ien Wu to move the waters
     of the sea.[8]
Though the Queen Mother's peach blossoms
     have bloomed red a thousand times,[9]
Ancestor P'eng and Shaman Hsien have died
     countless deaths.[10]

A piebald horse with blue-black hair mottled
     with patterns of coins,
Delicate spring willows savor the fine mist.

The zither-player coaxes me to the gold beaker
     with curved handles;
Spirit and blood yet unformed, my self asks,
     "Who is it?"

No need to drink wildly or to sing of fidelity
     to Governor Ting;[11]
In this world heroes have never had liege lords.
I will buy silk to embroider for the Lord of
     P'ing-yüan;[12]
What wine I have is only for libation on the
     earth in the state of Chao.[13]

The water clock urges water to choke the
     jade toad;[14]

> Lady Wei's hair has become so thin it can
>   hardly bear a comb.[15]
> Having seen autumn brows supplant fresh green,
> How can a young man of twenty be fretful?
>
> [p. 36]

Perhaps this is one of the long songs that "burst through" Li Ho's coat-flap. The first four lines depict changes in the world and the transience of life in comparison with immortality. In this vast overview of space and time, nothing endures but mutability and nothing is certain but the uncertainty of life. Even those who lived fabulously long lives, like Shaman Hsien and Ancestor P'eng, bear no comparison for longevity with the immortal Queen Mother's peach blossoms, let alone an ordinary mortal. Doomed to such a short life, what can, what will one do?

In the next four lines the poet suggests an answer: seek pleasures and enjoy life while it is Spring and while you are young. However, he goes on to ask: Can I, Li Ho, afford to look for momentary pleasures at the cost of my momentary life? My life, dwelling in this delicate body, is but a muddy mass of spirit and blood; before my true character is firmly shaped, how can I abandon myself to pleasure?

Thus, in lines nine through twelve, he proclaims his determination, his high resolve. There has been no way for him to see the emperor, and he has been drowning his sorrows in wine, but now he announces that, after all, there is no need to continue in this way, because in the world heroes have never had proper lieges. This explanation, however, affords him only momentary comfort. A hero may not have a master to serve, but still he will long for a lord who recognizes his talents. Although life is short, still there is time for him to revise his decision and worship a "Lord of P'ing-yüan," hoping that one day he will be singled out and given a chance to serve.

In the last four lines the poet becomes more conscious of the passing of time. Unlike the swift wind of the first line leveling mountains into plains, time's mutability is now perceived in miniature: in a moment a young lady's glossy hair and youthful eyebrows have become thin and scattered like falling leaves in the autumn wind. With time passing so fast, how can a man of twenty fret his life away?[16]

The poem above creditably expresses the fretful apprehensions of

an ambitious mind in a self-consoling and self-assuring voice. The
following poem also expresses the sorrow of such a frustrated mind,
with special reference to the pressures of time:

Autumn Comes

The paulownia wind startles the heart, strong
    men grieve;
Lamplight fading, a spinner cries her wintry silk.[17]
Who will see in green bamboo strips a roll of writings[18]
And not let silverfish moth them to powdery
    nothingness?

Thought-pulled, tonight my bowels must become
    straight!
Rain-cold, a fragrant spirit laments the littérateur:
In the autumn graveyard, ghosts chant Pao
    Chao's poems;[19]
Rancorous blood, a thousand years in the earth,
    turns emerald.

[pp. 36–37]

This is perhaps one of the short songs that "cut off" Li Ho's white
hair. When autumn comes, the wind rustles among paulownia trees;
stricken by the sound, the heart of an ambitious man is at first
surprised and then sinks in grief: time waits for no man, but hastens
the coming of his dotage before he can accomplish anything. Now,
the poet, alone in the fading light, writes and sings his sorrowful
songs, while a cricket-like insect (the "spinner") cries incessantly,
like a wheel spinning silk threads on a cold autumn night. The poet
singing songs is the spinner spinning silk threads; to combine these
two images, Li Ho creates a new term "han-su," which can be either
taken literally as cold white silk, the product of spinning, or as "cold
autumn," the time of spinning. I think both meanings are suggested
at the same time because in the next line, a string of green bamboo
strips, i.e., writings, suggests both the results of singing songs and
of spinning silk threads. However, the dominant worry in the poet's
mind is: who in the world will read and cherish my writings, even
though they are written with the heart's blood?

Possessed by such thoughts, the poet's heart is broken. The
Chinese cliché for "heartbroken" is "intestine-broken" (tuan-ch'ang)
or "sad intestines tied into a hundred knots" (ch'ou-ch'ang po-

chieh); but here, instead of repeating the cliché, Li Ho breaks new ground in the use of poetic language, creating a grotesque expression unique in Chinese traditional poetic sensibility: pulled by his thoughts, his intestines must become straight, implying that his intestines have been entangled with sorrow all the time.

Concern for the immortality of one's works is common to all artists; when Li Ho is in sorrow, an empathetic "fragrant spirit" of a writer from the past comes to lament with him. Judging from the context, I think "fragrant spirit" here refers to a departed man of letters rather than a lady's departed spirit; the word "fragrance" *(hsiang)* is meant to suggest the "fragrance of books" *(shu-hsiang)* rather than the perfumed scent of women. Although a poet suffers and is often neglected while alive, his most painstakingly constructed works are so moving that ghosts appreciate them and chant them at night. The heart's blood with which he writes is so full of rancor that it congeals into emerald jade after a thousand years, suggesting both the profundity and perpetuity of his emotions. Again, Li Ho breaks new ground in his expression of the artist's bitterness at frustrated ambition.

From the four poems discussed above, we have been able to perceive some aspects of Li Ho's mind: his grief, his ambitious desires, his anxiety and his rancor, as well as the fretfulness and loneliness that saturate many of his poems. The pressure of time on his mind runs through these four poems as a leitmotif. It seems that the pressure increases in proportion to the extent of adversity and ill-health, and is capable of crushing his heart at any given moment. Time itself often becomes a dominant concern in Li Ho's poems.

Song: Endless Past

The White Light returns to the western mountains;
The Jasper Flower rises far, far!
Where will the past and the present end?
Thousands of years have flown with the wind.
Sea-sands changed into rocks,
Fish-bubbles blown at the Ch'in bridge.[20]
The lights in the void drift in the beyond;
The pillars of bronze wear away with the years.[21]

[p. 45]

This poem expresses the endlessness of time as well as the

evanescence and eternal change in the world during the course of time. The White Light (the sun) and the Jasper Flower (the moon) shine one after the other; as day follows night, time goes on forever. By asking *where* will past and present end, and by describing a *scene* of the changing world, Li Ho presents an eternal *landscape* of time. Scenes depicting the world's mutability appear almost invariably in his poems concerning time. In "Vast Song," we find "The south wind blows away mountains . . ." and here reflects a contrast between the eternal and the transient. The stone bridge built by the Emperor of Ch'in in order to view the eternal sun rising from the sea, is now in ruins, indicating the crumbling of the human desire for immortality harbored by an emperor, yet the sun continues its cycles. The pillars of bronze symbolize Emperor Wu's desire for immortality, and they, too, wear away with the years. The only constant in this inconstant world is that of the lights in the void, which drift on and on. In Chinese *k'ung-kuang* (sky or empty light) can be taken literally as the lights in the sky, referring to "the White Light" and "the Jasper Flower," but it can also stand for time, similar to *kuang-yin* (light-shade). Only time, symbolized by the revolving sun and moon, goes on without end; all other things, sooner or later, are bound to drift with the wind and disappear.

Another poem similar in motif is entitled "Drums in the Capital Streets."

> At dawn their roaring hastens the turning sun;
> At dusk their roaring calls the moon out.
> In the Imperial City yellow willows reflect the new curtains;
> At the cypress mausoleum Flying Swallow's fragrant bones
>   lie buried.[22]
> The beat sounds thousands of years, the sun forever white;
> Emperor Wu and the Emperor of Ch'in can't hear them.[23]
> Granted, your raven hair turns the color of rush flowers;
> They alone, with the South Mountain, will guard the
>   Middle Kingdom.[24]
>
> No matter how many times Immortals have been buried
>   in Heaven;
> The sound of the water clock, on and on, will never
>   have cause to end.
>   [p. 134]

This poem describes the heartless passage of time. Symbolized by the beat of the drums, time rolls on as the sun and the moon follow each other day and night. As time passes, birth and death continue to take place. In the capital, spring willows brush against the newly changed curtains, implying the declaration of a new imperial consort, while at the cypress mausoleum, the former queen, like the Han beauty Flying Swallow, is laid to rest.

Time rolls on and on. Emperor Wu of Han and the Emperor of Ch'in, both enthusiastic seekers after the elixir of life, were doomed to failure, and can no longer hear the drums of time which beat out the measure of life in steady, unremitting cadences. It is time that outlasts all human life, and only the drums of time can persist along with the eternal South Mountain, keeping guard over China. Usually the Chinese think that to become an immortal is to overcome death, but here Li Ho thinks that time overcomes not only death but even supposed "immortality." Thus Li Ho develops new concepts of time and death: death is endless because time is endless. The Chinese Methuselahs, Ancestor P'eng and Shaman Hsien, will die countless deaths, and "immortals" in Heaven will be buried countless times, as long as time relentlessly continues.

Though Li Ho feels a sense of time's oppression, on occasion his reaction is not submissive but hostile, even defiant, as in the following poem:

Song: The Sun Rising

The white sun goes down Mount K'un-lun,[25]
Radiates light as if unravelling silk.
It shines only on sunflowers' hearts;
It will not shine on a wanderer's sorrow.

Curve upon curve, the Yellow River winds;
The sun rotates through the center.
My ears have heard of Daylight Valley;[26]
My eyes have never seen the Sunglow Tree.[27]

Melt rocks—I can't help it—
But why consume men?
When Yi bent his bow and shot his arrow,[28]
Why didn't he hit its foot
And make it forever unable to run?
Why make it bright at dawn and dark at dusk?

[p. 108]

Although the title indicates the sun rising, the poem begins with a description of the sun setting; thus the swift elapsing of time is suggested. The setting sun in the west resembles a white ball of silk threads. It radiates light as if unravelling silk. The sun merely shines on sunflowers, which turn their faces upward when the sun rises and down when the sun sets. The sunflower has traditionally been considered as a symbol of a vassal's loyalty to his lord.[29] If we take the sun as a symbol of the emperor, the sunflowers stand for his loyal subjects. However, the sun has a saddening effect on those travelers who wander alone, grieving at sunset that they still have a long way to go. As long as there is a sun, there will be wanderers; as long as there are wanderers, there will be sadness; therefore, it is the sun that saddens a wanderer, unsympathetic to his feelings. How heartless is the sun that hastens human lives to their end! Although the Yellow River flows swiftly, it turns once every thousand miles and only after nine turns runs into the sea. The sun in a single day rises from Daylight Valley, goes straight across the sky, down to the Sunglow Tree in the west, faster by far than running water! In this way, Li Ho goes a step further than Confucius' observation that "Time passes on like running water, not ceasing day or night!"[30] Had the sun been shot in the foot by Yi, the great archer, it would have been crippled and unable to run, time would have slowed its pace, and human beings could have enjoyed long lives and not had to rush restlessly about day and night. The poet faults the sun for not only melting rocks, but also for consuming men, who are not insensible. Time is no longer an impassive flow, but the active tool of the sun. In a poem entitled "Suffering from the Shortness of Days" (K'u chou tuan), Li Ho expressed himself in a similar vein.

> I do not know that the blue sky is high,
>   the yellow earth is thick;
> I only see the moon's cold and the sun's
>   heat come to burn human lifetimes.
>
> [p. 96]

Li Ho then rages against the six legendary dragons that draw the chariot of the sun, the vehicle of onrushing time.

> I will cut off the dragons' feet, chew the dragons' flesh,
> So that they can't turn back in the morning or lie down at night;
> Left to themselves the old won't die; the young won't cry.
>
> [p. 96]

Li Ho's hostility to time calls to mind the nineteenth-century French Symbolist poet Charles Baudelaire's lines:

> —O douleur! ô douleur! Le Temps mange la vie,
> Et l'obscur Ennemi qui nous ronge le coeur
> Du sang que nous perdons croît et se fortifie![31]

It seems that when Li Ho, the sufferer, sinks into the depths of misery or is oppressed by ruthless time, his mind often breaks free of the yoke of reality and escapes into a world of fantasy. To use traditional Chinese terminology, sometimes his *hun* (ethereal spirit) soars on a journey to Heaven, and sometimes his *p'o* (physical spirit) descends to the nether world,[32] resulting in two distinct types of setting in his poems—a world of brightness and light and one of darkness and gloom. The following example portrays his imaginary journey to Heaven.

Dreaming of Heaven

> The old hare and the shivering toad weep
> sky color.[33]
> The cloud-tower half open, walls oblique, white.
> The jade wheel crushes the dew: a wet sphere
> of light.
> Phoenix and jade pendants meeting on the cassia-
> fragrant path.[34]
>
> Yellow dust, clear water, below the Three
> Mountains;[35]
> Change upon change, a thousand years, like
> galloping horses.
> Seen from afar, the Middle Kingdom, nine spots
> in the mist;[36]
> One clear stream of ocean water pouring
> into a cup.

[pp. 27–28]

In this vision of Heaven, the newly risen moon is half-covered by clouds and the sky is colored by tears shed by the old hare and the shivering toad in the moon. Alternatively, the hare and the toad are weeping over the gloomy color of the sky. Later, the moon hangs in the middle of the sky like a jade wheel, rolling and crushing the dewdrops while absorbing their moisture and becoming a sphere of light. All these lunar visions are observed by the poet as he arrives on the moon, where he presumably meets the lunar goddess, Ch'ang-o. In the next four lines the poet looks down on this world and sees the swift and endless changes that run like galloping horses or "a galloping horse lantern" *(tsou ma teng),* a lantern adorned with a circle of paper horses which revolves when stimulated by the heat of the light. Revolving endlessly, it is a symbol of the vicissitudes of life.[37] Here the poet expresses his understanding of the relativity of time and space, probably derived from the *Chuang-tzu.*[38] It takes thousands of years to change mountains and waters in this world while, observed from the heavens, change is as swift as a horse's galloping or the turns of a ring of paper around a lantern. The nine states of China look like nine spots in the mist, and an ocean appears no more than a cup of water.

In another poem Li Ho describes the leisurely life in Heaven.

A Ballad of Heaven

> The River of Heaven turns at night,
>   drifts and whirls the stars;
> On the silver shore, the floating clouds
>   imitate the sound of water.
> The Jade Palace's cassia blossoms haven't
>   fallen yet.
> Handmaidens of the immortals gather fragrance,
>   girdle tassels dangling.
>
> The Princess of Ch'in rolls up her screen,
>   north window at dawn,[39]
> Paulownia trees planted before the window,
>   the green phoenixes are small.
> Prince Ch'iao plays his jade-pipes long as
>   goose-quills,[40]
> Calling out dragons to plough the mist and
>   plant magic herbs.
>
> Pink seal-ribbons of roseate clouds, white
>   skirts of lotus-silk,
> Take a walk on Green Isle, gathering orchid
>   blossoms: Spring.[41]
> Pointing to the east, Hsi Ho really can gallop
>   his horses![42]
> Sea-dust forms anew below the stone mountains.

[p. 35]

The poem begins with a distant spectacular view of Heaven. The River of Heaven (the Milky Way) turns, drifting and whirling its stars like a watery current, while floating clouds, like water, flow along the banks of the starry stream with a gurgling sound. Not far from the river lies the Jade Palace of the moon, where the cassia tree is in flower and fairy maidens are gathering fragrant blossoms. The next six lines depict the immortals' daily life in Heaven. The Princess of Ch'in amuses herself by playing the *hsiao* flute, as she used to do before she ascended to Heaven. Perhaps the paulownia tree in front of her window is still young, so only small phoenixes come to sit on it. Prince Ch'iao, although immortal, still has to work: he calls out dragons to plough clouds and plant magic herbs to ensure continued immortality. Sometimes the immortals descend to the Green Isle to walk and pick orchid blossoms. The poem ends with another scene of earthly change.

In contrast to his "ethereal spirit" which ascends to Heaven, Li Ho's "physical spirit" often descends to the nether world. Let us take the following poem as an example:

Exhortation No. 3

The South Mountain: how sad it is!
Ghostly rain sprinkles the empty grass.
Ch'ang-an, midnight, Autumn;
Before the winds, how many men have aged?
Dim and dark the evening path,
Curling upward the bluish oaks by the road.
The moon at its zenith, trees without shadows—
The whole mountain only white dawn.
Lacquer torches welcome the newcomer,
In the secluded field, fireflies flit pell-mell.

[p. 69]

Lamenting that time and tide hasten men to death, the poet pictures to himself the final scene of one's life. The setting is South Mountain to the south of Ch'ang-an, and here as elsewhere in China, the graveyards are situated on the mountain slopes to avoid flood damage. How mournful is the graveyard here when ghostly rain drizzles on the desolate grass! The poet creates a new term, "ghostly rain," which is probably meant to suggest cold, quiet, drizzling rain in the graveyard, with barely visible ghosts emerging from a misty distance. In Ch'ang-an, the prosperous, populous capital, are assembled all kinds of people, of high and low social position, rich and poor. But the poet asks how many of them have grown old in the face of these winds that blow daily across the hills and grow chilly in autumn. No man remains unchanged by time and the great cycles as symbolized by these natural forces. The dawn which breaks over this funereal scene carries its load of irony, because for the newcomer there will be no more dawns. The term "newcomer" itself reinforces this irony because in common usage the term *hsin-jen* usually means bride. South Mountain is no more a mountain of this world, but becomes a realm of the shades, where the torches welcoming the new arrival remind us that life is as brief and as evanescent as the light of the fireflies rushing hither and thither.

In this poem Li Ho draws a detailed picture of joining the dead when his spirit would become a will-o'-the-wisp wandering in the secluded wilds. There is an implication, because of the welcoming party, that his soul will no longer suffer and feel lonely. Whether Li Ho really believed he could find companionship after death is difficult to ascertain. However, the thought of Su Hsiao-hsiao,[43] a lovely courtesan who died young and waited in the other world for her lover, certainly occupied his mind at least once:

Song of Su Hsiao-hsiao

Dark orchid dew
Like tearful eyes;
Nothing with which to knot two hearts;
Misty flowers cannot bear cutting.

Grass as a cushion,
Pinetree as a canopy;
The wind for clothing,
The waters for jade-pendants;
In the varnished carriage
Long waiting;
A cold emerald candle
Consuming its light.

Below West Mound,
Wind and rain blow.

[p. 27]

This is a poem on Su Hsiao-hsiao's rendezvous after death with her lover, inspired by a *yüeh-fu* song with the same title:

> I ride in a varnished carriage;
> You ride on a piebald horse.
> Where do we knot our two hearts?
> At West Mound, below the pine and cypress.[44]

Here the poet imagines a most pathetic scene at Su Hsiao-hsiao's grave. The dewdrops sprinkled on the secluded orchid are like her eyes full of tears. While in life, she and her lover vowed to die and be buried together, their hearts tied in a lovers' knot. But now after her death, nothing is left; with what can she bind their hearts? The misty flowers close by are as frail as she; how can they be cut and sent to her lover as a token of love? After death, there are only tears brimming in her eyes while she waits for her lover to join in her fate. Then, the poet *seems* to visualize Su Hsiao-hsiao waiting for her lover in front of the grave. She sits on a grass-cushion, under a pine-canopy; the wind blows as her transparent dress waves, and the gurgling water around the grave sounds like the tinkling of jade on her girdle-tassels or pendants. She used to ride in her varnished carriage, but now she sits, waiting. The line "a cold emerald candle" carries with it ambiguities which focus this poem.[45] One line of interpretation is that the spirit of Su Hsiao-hsiao actually waits in this desolate scene. Another is that the entire poem is ironic—really nothing is there, and only the imaginative force of a desirous lover could find eyes in orchid dew, see grass as a cushion, and wind as clothing. If such a lover's imagination were strong enough, he might believe that a candle of the spirit-world would burn with a cold emerald flame as easily as he could imagine that the spirit of his deceased beloved awaits him. In this sense the line can be read as a poignant oxymoron. If, on the other hand, a lover were disappointed at finding nothing by the grave mound, his hopes would be extinguished, like a cold green candle with no flame. This brings us back to the preceding lines. Is it perhaps the living lover who has come in a varnished carriage and waits for a vision of his loved one, only to have his hopes sputter like "a cold emerald candle consuming its own light," and to be left, in the end, with nothing but wind and rain below the grave mound?

So far I have discussed only the darker side of Li Ho's poetry:

those poems tinged with or related to his longing, his disappointment, his hostility against time, his celestial dreams, his visions of
the world beyond the grave; in short, his personal experiences and
fantasies. Most of those poems are gloomy, dolorous, and somber: in
his own words, "a cold emerald candle" glimmering in the wild
darkness. However, as I mentioned at the beginning of this brief
essay, Li Ho's mind has a brighter side which belongs to day rather
than night, although at times the sun does not shine in this world. In
these poems the poet is less the sufferer and more the observer
whose themes range from social events to divine spirits and aesthetic
experience. These poems will be discussed in the second part of this
chapter.

II   *Dreary Visions in the Broad Light of Day*

As a poetic observer, Li Ho also wrote many poems which can be
divided into five major varieties according to subject matter: (1)
poems of social comment; (2) poems on historical subjects; (3) poems
about women; (4) descriptive poems; (5) poems about divine spirits.
As a whole, these poems exhibit two different tendencies: (1) didactic: out of the poet's sympathy for sufferers or his righteous indignation at social injustice; (2) aesthetic: expressing the poet's personal
aesthetic experiences. Generally speaking, poems commenting on
social conditions tend to be didactic while poems describing scenes
or objects tend to be aesthetic; poems on other subjects can be
either didactic or aesthetic.

I.   *Social Comment*
Exhortation No. 1

Ho-p'u has no more shining pearls,[46]
Lung-chou has no more "wood slaves":[47]
These suffice to prove that Nature's fecundity
Cannot meet the magistrate's needs.
The woman of Yüeh had not begun to weave,
Silkworms of Wu had just started wriggling
When a district official came on horseback,
His face ferocious with barbellated purple whiskers.
From his bosom he brought out a square board;
On the board were several lines of words.

"Were it not for the magistrate's anger,
Would I have visited your hovel?"

The woman of Yüeh bowed to the district official:
"The mulberry sprouts are still small now;
You have to wait until late Spring,
Only then will the silk reels spin and turn . . ."

While the woman of Yüeh was putting it into words,
Her husband's sister treated him to yellow millet.
The district official gorged the meal and left,
Then the revenue officer arrived at the house to boot.

[p. 68]

This is a poem on the people's suffering from heavy, endless taxes
and the greediness of government officials. Ho-p'u used to be a
major pearl center, but by now the officials have grabbed up all the
pearls. Lung-chou suffers from a like fate and produces no more
oranges. These two facts suffice to prove that even nature fails to
gratify a magistrate's rapacity. Here lies the didactic theme of the
poem. To support the argument, the poet provides a dramatic situation: a country woman's dealings with a district official. Knowing
that the official is making an unreasonable demand, a demand he
falsely attributes to the magistrate, the woman, with a genial attitude, offers a sensible excuse while her sister-in-law serves good
food. No sooner has the district official gone away than a revenue
officer comes to demand other tax duties.

This poem is very similar to Tu Fu's "Shih-hao Official" (*Shih-hao
li*), both in theme and in tone.

The Official at Shih-hao Village

At dusk when I lodge at Shih-hao Village,
There is an official capturing men in the night.
The old man climbs the wall and runs;
The old woman goes out the gate to look.
What fury in the official's shout!
What bitterness in the old woman's sobs!
I hear her go forward and make her speech:
"My three sons are in Yeh-ch'eng to guard the frontier.
One son enclosed a letter to me:
The other two just died in battle.
Those who survive somehow live by their wits;
Those who have died are finished forever.

In the house there isn't another man.
There's only a grandson at the breast.
My grandson's mother hasn't left us yet.
Indoors or out she hasn't a whole skirt.
Although I'm an old woman and my strength has faded,
Please let me go back with you to night, sir,
To answer the urgent call for du.y at Ho-yang.
At least I'm able to prepare the morning meals."
The night is late, the speaking voice breaks off.
I seem to hear choked, hidden weeping.
At daybreak, I go ahead on my journey,
Taking leave only of the old man.[48]

While Tu Fu describes the inhuman conscription of men into service in time of war, Li Ho's poem portrays merciless government levies in peacetime, but both are concerned with the people's suffering under official oppression. However the poetic viewpoint of each is quite different. Tu Fu's poem begins with the poet's coming to Shih-hao village and ends with his leaving. It describes an episode seen and heard by the poet who himself appears in the poem, although he does not intervene in the conflict, and the reader hears what T.S. Eliot calls the poet's second voice.[49] However, in Li Ho's poem, the poet acts as an observer: from beginning to end, he hides behind the characters in his poems and only his third voice is heard.

In Tu Fu's poem the poet's attention is focused on the situation created in the lives of the villagers and their response to the arrival of the conscription officer. The official is defined in abstract terms, heard but not seen, his demeanor discernible only through the quality of his voice. But an account is given of every member of the family: the old man who ran away and his old wife; the three sons on the frontier; and the grandson at his mother's breast, as if to convince the official, and the reader, that there are no other men in the house. In Li Ho's poem, however, the district official is dominant among the *dramatis personae* and is presented by the poet in three different postures, with a close-up description of his savage visage befitting a harsh official. He arrives in a fury, his whiskers fringing his face like a ferocious dragon, he acts pompously in his official role to justify his awkward position in making unreasonable demands of the villagers, and finally he leaves after crudely gorging the millet in animal fashion. Only the woman of Yüeh and her sister-in-law come out to deal with the official, suggesting tacitly that all the men, if any, have already "climbed the wall and run away" or have been called up to guard the frontier.

At the end of Tu Fu's poem, the old man returns to his own house after the official has taken away the old woman, and probably their daughter-in-law and grandson have already run away: all these consequences are suggested by the admirable last line. However, since the old man returns to his house and the official has left, one can sense a temporary peace before another similar round of trouble. In Li Ho's poem, no sooner has the district official left than a revenue officer arrives: the officials never stop bothering the people, whose suffering is endless.

As far as the didactic objectives are concerned, Tu Fu's poem attacks the mercilessness of the official who does not even show leniency to a feeble old woman, while Li Ho aims at the official's unbounded desires, which even nature fails to satisfy. The world Tu Fu explores in his poem is within the realm of human affairs, or the conflict between the people and officials, while Li Ho's world has exceeded human affairs and extended to nature, touching upon the eternal conflict between human desires and nature's productivity.

Let us now examine another didactic poem by Li Ho.

The Song of an Old Jade-hunter

Hunt for jade! Hunt for jade! Water-emeralds only!
Carved into "Sway-as-she-walks" hair-ornaments just for the
  love of beauty.
The old man hungry, cold, dragons become sorrowful:
In Indigo Stream, water vapor has never been white and clear.[50]

Night rain on the high hill, he eats hazelnuts;
The blood in a cuckoo's mouth—the old man's tears.[51]
Indigo Stream's water is satiated with living men;
Bodies dead a thousand years still hate the stream's water.

Slanting mountain, cypress in the wind, rain falls like
  whistling;
At the foot of a spring, a greenish rope hangs swirling.
The village cold, the hut white, he worries about his
  pampered infant;
The ancient terrace, the stone steps, the bowel-hanging grass.

[pp. 53-54]

Officials belabor the people to hunt for jade at the cost of their
lives to satisfy the vanity of court favorites. The repetition in the first
line indicates the incessant labor of the people as well as the endless
demands of the officials. The only kind of jade good enough to satisfy
the officials is water emerald, which, carved into a hair-ornament,
makes a woman more attractive when she walks. However, in
hunting for jade, the old man suffers from cold and hunger; it rains
on the mountain slopes at night and he has only hazelnuts to eat.
Even dragons in the stream sympathize with his plight and become
sad, bothered also by the disturbing effects of the man's efforts in
the water in which they live. The bitterness in the old man's heart,
when it wells up with tears, becomes like blood in the mouth of a
crying cuckoo.

It is in such dangerous work that numerous jade-hunters have
fallen over the precipice into the stream, which has already grown
tired of consuming human lives. Those who have died seem to
direct their rancor against the stream's water rather than against the
officials; this of course is an irony. I think the poem may well have
ended here if the poet had wanted only to admonish the officials.
However, the poet gives an impressive close-up describing the old
man's state of mind while risking his life in the search for jade.

On the slanting mountain, the wind blows among cypresses and
the rain whistles: a storm is raging. The trees on the mountain are
blown aslant, creating the illusion that the mountain itself is slanted.
Cypresses are usually found by graves and hence are suggestive of
the shadow of death, a gloomy foreboding of impending tragedy.
From the spring-dripping rocks hangs a greenish rope with which
the old man gets down to the stream. At the end of the rope dangling and swirling against the cliff, hangs the old man, or more
precisely, the old man's precarious life itself. The old man knows
that at any moment he could sink into the water, his grave, and he
worries about his beloved child left at home in a thatched hut. As he
dangles and swirls with the rope, the ancient terrace, the stone
steps, and the "bowel-hanging grass" pass before his dazed eyes.
His heart is broken, and so is what he sees. The last line, a succes-
sion of three nouns without any verbs, suggests such a broken feeling. Moreover, it is charged with highly symbolic meanings. The
"bowel-hanging grass" is also called "child-worrying vine" (ssu-tzu
man) or "parting grass" (li-pieh ts'ao); therefore it suggests at least
three kinds of feeling in the old man: a) his sadness; b) his affection
for his child; c) his premonition of death.

As I have said above, Li Ho expresses his sadness in such a characteristic way as his intestines being tugged straight, but here he goes one step further: the intestines are hanging straight as the old man's life hangs on a rope. This image suggests a kind of extreme, desperate sadness. In addition, the bowel-hanging grass is juxtaposed with the ancient terrace and the stone steps, possibly a historic site or a park with a tower or a pavilion. If so, the ironic contrast between the apprehensions suggested by the bowel-hanging grass and the leisurely peaceful mood suggested by the terrace is striking.

Wei Ying-wu (ca. 735–ca. 835), a poet earlier than Li Ho by about fifty years, has a similar poem:

Song: Hunting for Jade

> The Government drafts young men,
> Says, "Hunt for Indigo Stream jade!"
> On the summit of the mountain no other men at night;
> Under the thick hazels they take shelter while it rains.
> The solitary woman back from sending food,
> Sadly, sadly cries to the south of her house.[52]

Comparing these two poems, we find that Wei's poem conveys only a general impression of the event, while Li Ho's penetrates the old jade-hunter's actual sutuation, is much more concrete in description, and explores the old man's sadness in greater depth. Almost every line in Li Ho's poem is weightier, graver in its depiction of a jade-hunter's suffering, because it focuses on the experiences of one individual in his final extremity, and thus it creates a kind of intensity that is lacking in Wei's poem. The extreme situation set up in Li Ho's poem has the following features: (1) instead of saying "young men" in general, it depicts a particular old man as a model and suggests that, old as he is, he has to hunt for jade because all his young sons have already died in this dangerous work; (2) instead of saying "no other men" on the top of the mountain at night, it makes the Indigo Stream complain that its water has grown tired of living men; (3) instead of "taking shelter under the thick hazels," the old man suffers from cold in the stormy night; (4) instead of having someone to send him food, the old man eats wild hazelnuts to assuage his hunger; (5) instead of "crying sadly," the old man's tears are like blood in a cuckoo's mouth. Moreover, Li Ho's poem directs its arrow of indignation toward the officials who try to win their favorites' hearts at the cost of the jade-hunters' lives. Wei's poem lacks such a critical tone, although it also suggests that some jade-hunters have met their ends—that is why the solitary woman cries after sending food to her husband who has already fallen into the stream. However, "to cry" in Wei's poem is no more than an expression of one's sadness that lasts only temporarily. Transcending the state of sadness, Li Ho's poem expresses the hatred that continues throughout all time, that continues even after death. His dead jade-hunters' hatred is directed against the stream rather than against the officials: the implication is that there is no way to voice their complaint, which makes it all the more bitter and poignant.

Li Ho's poems on current events also frequently take a didactic tone, forcefully pointing an accusatory finger at the government.

The Caves of the Huang Family

> With a sparrow's tread, hopping on the sand with a
> quick-quick sound;
> Horn bows four feet in length, arrowheads of green
> stone.
> Black banners dip three times, bronze drums sound;
> They utter shrill apes' cries, shaking their quivers.
>
> Variegated cloth binds their shanks, widths arranged
> at a half-slant;
> By the riverbank they swarm in squads, reflecting the
> arrowroot flowers.
> In mountain tarns, under night mist, white crocodiles
> growl;
> Bamboo snakes and flying insects spit golden sand.
> Leisurely driving bamboo horses, at ease, they
> go home;[53]
> The government troops on their own kill the natives of
> Jung-chou.[54]

                                                          [p. 55]

The aboriginal tribes in present-day Kwangsi province lived in caves and belonged to the Huang family during the T'ang dynasty. They often rebelled against the central government. Three major rebellions were recorded in Li Ho's lifetime: the first, in 794 when Li Ho was five years old, the second, in 808 when he was nineteen, and the third, in 816, the year he died. This poem was probably written in 808 immediately after the second rebellion. At any rate, it describes the barbarians' particular gait and weapons, their flag-signaling operations and lively martial spirit, their war outfits and ranks as well as their tactics. The arrowroot flowers are reddishly purple; when the barbarians swarm in squads by the riverbank, their sun-burned complexions reflect this ruddy color. In their nocturnal forays for plunder, they are compared to snarling white alligators overthrowing fishing boats. They shoot arrows like bamboo snakes or like flying insects spitting out golden sand with poison. Finally, in the last two lines the poet draws a striking contrast between the aboriginal tribes' calmness after victory and the government troops' cruelty and contemptibility: defeated by the native warriors, they kill the native civilians in order to claim credit and be rewarded by the court. In the last line the government troops' ineptitude and avidity for rewards, the natives' innocence, as well as the aboriginal tribes' valor are all implied.

Li Ho has written eleven poems entitled "Exhortation" *(kan-feng)* (pp. 68–70 and 142–144), in which a didactic theme is intended although not necessarily explicitly stated. In many of the poems on the quest after Taoist immortality, his satirical barbs are directed against the futility of this enterprise. He derides those immortality-seekers who would make gold by smelting cinnabar, but who get nothing more than "purple mist" (p. 51). In Taoist alchemy a turtle, after eating a certain amount of cinnabar, was believed to be able to change into a snake riding the white mist. However, Li Ho transforms this concept into an unpleasant and spiteful image: "With eight trigrams on its back it is called immortal;/ Its noxious scales and stubborn armor slippery with fishy spittle!" (p. 109)

Sometimes Li Ho directed his satirical criticism against the reigning Emperor Hsien-tsung who, like Emperor Wu of Han and the first Emperor of Ch'in, assiduously sought immortality through the alchemical arts. As criticizing the emperor's favorite almost amounts to criticizing the emperor himself, Li Ho's admonition of the futility of this pursuit in fact could have endangered his life.[55]

Another aspect of Li Ho's satirical criticism is reflected in his poems on current events, especially on the extravagant pleasure-seeking of powerful personages at court. His deliberate and lavish descriptions of their indulgence in luxury and carnal pleasures often carry mixed feelings of satirical criticism and barely concealed envy.

In a poem entitled "Pleasures of a Princess' Armored Outing"
(*Kuei-chu cheng-hsing lo*) (p. 56), the satire is directed at a princess
of the time who traveled to a banquet in Ho-yang accompanied by
her retinue and a "rosy jade general of cavalry" who, attired in
golden armor, carried perfumed staves and silk banners, mimicking
the military men of the day. In "A Song of General Lü" *(Lü
Chiang-chün ko)* (p. 129), he attacks the "powdered lady general,"
the eunuch-commander T' u-t' u Ch' eng-ts'ui, who prevented military advisers from getting the ear of the emperor, but who hid under
the flag when the rebel issued a challenge:

> The armored cavalry of Mount Heng calls for metal
> lances;
> From afar they smell the perfume of the florid arrows in
> the quiver.

> [p. 129]

III *Historical Subjects*

Along the line of impersonal poems, now let us turn to Li Ho's
poems on historical subjects.

Song of the Bronze Immortal Bidding
Farewell to Han

In the eighth month of the fifth year of the *Ch'ing-lung* period
(237)[56] of Emperor Ming of Wei *(regnet* 226–39), palace officials
were ordered to harness their carriages and go west to obtain the
statue of the Immortal holding a dew-plate commissioned by Emperor Hsiao-wu of Han *(regnet* 141–88 B.C.), in order to erect it in
front of the palace hall. When the palace officials had detached the
plate, the Immortal, while being put into the carriage, began to
shed copious tears. I, Li Ch'ang-chi, a descendant of the royal
princes of T'ang, have therefore written this "Song of the Bronze
Immortal Bidding Farewell to Han."

> Liu the Childe buried in Mao-ling, a passenger
> in the autumn wind;
> At night hearing horse-neighing, at dawn not
> a trace.
> By the painted balustrades, cassia trees hang
> autumn fragrance;

In the thirty-six palaces, earth-flowers are
emerald.

The officials of Wei harnessed their carriages,
pointing to a thousand miles;
The Eastern Pass's acid wind shoots the apple
of the eye.
Vainly, with the moon of Han, he went out the
palace gates;
Recalling the Emperor, his pure tears shed like
leaden water.

Withering orchids saw the guest off at the
Hsien-yang road;
If Heaven had feelings, Heaven, too, would
grow old.[57]
Carrying the dew-plate, he set out alone, the
moon bleak and desolate;
Wei City already far behind, the sound of the
waves grows faint.

[pp. 44–45]

This is a parting song, as the title and the preface indicate, written
by the poet on behalf of the Bronze Immortal when he leaves the
palace of Han. The statue towered two hundred feet, extending
seven *wei* (distance between two stretched arms) in circumference,
and was built by the Emperor Wu of Han who, great as he was,
believed in Taoist immortality. The Immortal holds a bronze plate
and a jade-cup overhead in the palms of his hands to catch dew from
the clouds. According to Taoist belief, the dew so caught, swallowed
together with small pieces of jade, can bring longevity. After the
Empire of Han was taken over by Wei (220) in the fifth year of the
Ch'ing-lung period (237), the statue was moved from Ch'ang-an, the
capital of Han, to Hsü-ch'ang, the capital of Wei, in modern Honan
province. Li Ho's poem is based on this historical event and expresses the Immortal's feelings on parting from the palace of Han.

The Emperor Wu of Han, one of the greatest emperors in
Chinese history and one of the most enthusiastic seekers of the elixir
of life, was buried in Mao-ling. The first line of the Immortal's song
seems to say that no matter how great he was, he proved but "a
passenger in the autumn wind," mortal like the rest of men. The
mysterious second line has given rise to three different interpreta-

tions: that at night the divine horses from Heaven come to receive Emperor Wu's departed spirit; or that his spirit makes a round of visits at night and the horses in the cortège whinny; or possibly that since Emperor Wu sent an expedition to Ferghana to obtain the best horses, those horses neighed at night after he died. But here I think the line suggests that Emperor Wu died discontented and his unyielding spirit, ambitious and heroic as ever, is still commanding his horses in battle at night.

The first two lines, then, express the idea that although the great Emperor Wu sought longevity, he inevitably died; his martial spirit, which had commanded his cavalry in battle, emerges at night, but in the morning disappears without leaving any trace. One hundred and fifty years after, when the Bronze Immortal was moved, Emperor Wu's palaces had already fallen into ruin and were overgrown with "earth-flowers": emerald-green moss. Even worse, the Bronze Immortal on whom he had relied to gain immortality now becomes a captive, taken by the officials of Wei who came "a thousand miles" from the new capital in the east. The wind blown from Eastern Pass (Han-ku Pass) is so "acid" that it assails the Immortal's eyes like an arrow. When the Immortal has to bid farewell to the Han palace where he has dwelt day and night for one hundred and fifty years, carrying with him the same bright moon as in the time of Han, he cannot help shedding copious tears. These tears from the bronze eroded by the acid air are as heavy and crystalline as leaden water. At this parting scene, only the fading orchids along the road of Hsien-yang, Ch'ang-an, silently bid farewell to this tearful "guest." Seeing such a scene and affected by such a parting sorrow, even Heaven, if it had feelings, would also feel sad and grow old! Holding his dew-plate, leaving his native place in loneliness, he now and then looks at the moon which, also ravaged by the wind, seems to grow bleak and desolate.

This deeply moving poem is one of Li Ho's best, mainly because of the world it explores and the way in which Li Ho expresses this exploration. The poem deals with one of the greatest human sorrows, that of mortality, and explores it by means of a basic sensory experience: shedding tears. The poem also succeeds in the way of expression: using the Bronze Immortal as an objective correlative and making the reader share the Immortal's feelings and sorrows. Li Ho achieves an artistic effect by making the Immortal seem as human as possible, shortening or eliminating the distance between a statue and a human being.

The first stanza evokes Emperor Wu's death and the ruin of his palaces, indicating that human life as well as the human world are vicissitudinous; herein lies one reason why the Immortal sheds tears, as developed in the second stanza. Psychologically, he is both grateful and ashamed of the master who created him and who entrusted him with his highest desire, longevity, which he has failed to help him obtain. On the other hand, he is sad about his master's, or his own, fortune: great and heroic as his master was, his demise proves that no life, no glory can last forever; even the life of the Immortal himself will finally succumb to the buffeting of the wind. The third stanza presents a dramatic scene of parting and expresses the theme of the poem: "If Heaven had feelings, Heaven would also grow old." Men suffer, precisely because they have feelings: with feelings, there are sorrows. Probably the greatest sorrow for human beings is separation by death. The Immortal, one hundred and fifty years old, is now captured and forced to leave his native palace to serve an emperor of a different dynasty, the successor of the usurper of his master's empire; to be sure, he would have died rather than betray his creator. And when he thinks of his master and his own future, he cannot help shedding tears. Such a sad situation, such pathos, certainly moves Heaven to tears; the moon thereupon becomes desolate and bleak. Li Ho called himself "a man fried by feelings" (*chien-ch'ing-jen*) and his facial features are not difficult to imagine:

> Bones thin, no color in his face,
> Disease rushing to his head, his sidelocks sparse.
>
> [pp. 58–59]

In fact, it is a face just as bleak and desolate as the pale moon is to the Immortal's tearful eyes.

The Emperor Wu of Han was an ambitious and heroic emperor. When he realized his ambition of success in government and in war, his drive for immortality arose in proportion to his worldly successes: his desire became that of living forever in glory and splendor. A poem on Emperor Wu touches upon his ambitious mind:

The K'un-lun Envoy

> No tidings from the K'un-lun envoy;
> At Mao-ling, misty trees bear sorrow's hue.

On the golden plate jade dew drips, drenches itself;
Primordial Spirit far and wide cannot be gathered.

On the unicorns' backs, the stone's patterns crack;
Beneath the dragons' scales, red limbs are broken.
Where is the willfully broken heart that aspired to
    ten thousand dominions?
In the middle of the sky, night long lingers the bright moon.
[p. 154, p. 151]

The K'un-lun envoy refers to Chang Ch'ien (?–114 B.C.), who was dispatched by Emperor Wu of Han to many countries in the Western Regions (*hsi-yü*, a general name for regions west of Tun-huang in the Han dynasty) to spread and promote the national glory of Han. However, before Chang Ch'ien returned from his mission, Emperor Wu's grave at Mao-ling had already been covered in gloomy mist, and he could not hear the report bearing the good news that his ambition for a greater empire had been fulfilled. The golden plate in the Immortal's palms has caught a large amount of dew, yet the emperor cannot be there to drink it; the Primordial Spirit, let loose in the vast universe, cannot be gathered and absorbed in order to obtain longevity. Another possible interpretation is that in order to obtain longevity, Emperor Wu has exhausted his own spirit, which, after he died, returns to the vast universe. Either way, Li Ho suggests Emperor Wu failed to gather the Primordial Spirit spreading far and wide between Heaven and earth and died unfulfilled. His tomb ruined, the stone statues of animals before his grave broken, where is the great hero now? Where in this world is the ambitious spirit that tried to subjugate ten thousand kingdoms? To his mortification, it lies beneath a mound of dust under the bright moon. The last line describes a natural scene that lasts forever and thus provides an eternal, ironic contrast to Emperor Wu's buried ambition.

IV *Poems About Women*

Among Li Ho's two hundred and forty-two poems there are about forty on women, making up one-sixth of the total. Whether or not Li Ho, as some critics believe,[58] died from sexual dissipation is a question impossible to answer. However, since he wrote so many poems about women, he indeed seems to have been "a troubador who sings of love" (*yen-ch'ing k'o*) as he called himself, or at least a man apt to be carried away by feelings for women, either out of love or sympathy. These poems fall into two major types: portraits of neglected palace girls or deserted women, the so-called *kung-yüan-shih* (palace-grievance poems) or *kuei-yüan-shih* (boudoir grievance poems); and aesthetic descriptions of woman's beauties, the so-called *yen-t'i-shih* (sensuous style poems).

Song of a Palace Doll

> Candlelight hung on high shines on gauze
>   emptiness;
> In flowery rooms at night cinnabar *gardes-cour*
>   are pounded.
>
> The elephant's mouth puffs incense, the woolen
>   rugs are warm;
> The Seven Stars hanging over the city wall
>   hear the night watch's clappers,
>
> Cold enters the eaves-nets, the palace shadows
>   darken;
> The colored phoenixes on the curtains' upper
>   borders bear frost-tracks.
> A crying mole-cricket mourns the moon under the
>   hooked balustrades;
> "Bend-your-knees" hinges and bronze doorknobs
>   lock in Ah-chen.
>
> "In dreams I enter the door of my house;
>   I walk the sandy isles;
> Where the River of Heaven falls is the
>   Long Island Road.
> I wish my Prince, luminous bright as the sun,
> Would let me go, riding on a fish slashing
>   the waves."

[p. 59]

This poem reveals the inward feeling of a palace maiden who stays alone waiting for the emperor's visit and longing for home in her disappointment. Under the candlelight shining through the gauze lampshade or curtain, someone is pounding cinnabar geckos. It was believed that when geckos were fed on more than seven catties of cinnabar, they became completely red; after these red geckos were pounded ten thousand times with a pestle, they became paste which was used to mark the bodies of the emperor's concubines. It was believed that the red marks on their bodies would disappear only when they had sexual intercourse. Geckos were called "palace guardians" *(shou-kung)* because they could thus guarantee the royal concubines' chastity. Now the poem does not indicate explicitly who is pounding geckos. If it is the palace girl herself, the second line can be interpreted this way: she pounds her own pigments to prove her faithfulness to the man she serves, or she occupies herself with such work lest she should sit idle, implying that she is waiting wholeheartedly only for the emperor's favor. If it is someone else, say a eunuch, pounding outside her room, then this line indicates that she is sad to hear the pounding noise, reflecting bitterly that she will never have need of it again. In the context of the whole, this line appears to suggest that the palace girl is confined and her sexual desire is frustrated. She can only wait, probably in vain, for the only one who has the power and the right to satisfy her longing. She heats the room; incense puffs from the mouth of an elephant-shaped censer; the woolen rug laid in front of the bed is thick and warm. But the emperor does not come.

She goes to bed; at midnight when the Big Dipper hangs over the city-wall, she still lies awake, listening to the sound of the watch's clappers. As night advances, the cold sneaks in through the eaves-nets and the phoenixes decorating the borders of the curtains are covered with frost. Outside her room, beneath the hooked balustrades, a crying mole-cricket mourns the moon, echoing the girl's inmost loneliness and disappointment. Now, again, she reviews her own situation: a neglected woman locked in the forbidden palace, who has never enjoyed the imperial favor, like Ah-chen, the discarded favorite of Emperor Wen of Wei *(regnet 220–26)*. Here, the hinges resemble bended knees that suggest humiliation to match the humiliating marks of the cinnabar geckos. Perhaps her pride stirs her human dignity, prompting her to rid herself of all restraints physical or spiritual which bind her to her perpetual state of lonely unfulfillment. In dreams, she returns to her home on the sandy isles, far beyond the other end of the Milky Way, probably the swampy regions south of the Yangtze River. Her fate is at the mercy of the emperor whom she beseeches: "Let me go, although my home is far, far away and there is no boat; if you let me go, I would happily ride on a fish and leave at once." The images in the last stanza are harmonious and logical. Her home is probably on an island surrounded by water and many other islets. The road leading there is connected by sandy isles, just as the River of Heaven is composed of many stars. Therefore, where the River of Heaven ends, the road to her home begins.

On her homeward journey through the River of Heaven, she rides on a fish—an image so quaint that a traditional commentator suspects that there might be some mistake in the text.[59] This marvelous image can be interpreted in many ways. Instead of a boat, she rides a fish because a fish is able to travel faster, thus showing the impatience of her longing for home. A palace girl can never be released, any more than she can really ride on a fish, but she is so obsessed with the thought of going home that in her unrealistic imaginings such things become possible. The fish is described as "slashing the waves" with its tail and fins, an energetic action indicating joy, or even gratitude, as if it were being returned to water after a long absence. The palace girl rides on the fish which wiggles with joy for her, welcoming and helping her as though she were also a fish taken out of water and kept in the palace for many years and now set free. In fact, her lord will never be so generous and humane as to let her go. What a pity that this human-fish from the lake region should die of thirst for water and love! In addition, this poem is full of contrasted images: dark and bright, day and night, cold and warm, the moon and the sun, outside and inside of the room, sadness and joy, human being and insect, far and near, land and water, road and river, islet and star, dream and reality, expectation and disappointment, palace girl and fish. It is not difficult to find ironic effects produced by such contrasts.

Li Ho wrote another rather obscure poem on a similar theme:

Hall after Hall

Hall after hall, again, hall after hall,
Red vanished, the plum's ashes fragrant.
Ten years powdery silverfish spawned on the painted beams;
A hungry worm would not eat, but sits pushing yellow,
   broken bits.
Orchid blossoms already old, peach leaves long;
In the forbidden garden, hanging blinds block the Imperial light.
In Hua-ch'ing hot springs, arsenic-stone waters.
Hovering around, white phoenixes follow the Emperor.

[pp. 59–60]

The title is the name of one of the *yüeh-fu* songs, but I think here it is used literally to indicate the successive halls of a palace where neglected and discarded concubines live alone. The first line with its repetitions suggests the emptiness of the halls as well as the loneliness of the concubine, and at the same time implies repeated sighs. Why does she sigh? The answer is in the second line, an obscure one which has puzzled many commentators. We need not identify "red" with a particular object like a red beam of plum wood, but take it simply as an objective correlative expressing emotions. "Red" refers to a woman's beauty or youth; the plum-blossom stands for a palace girl or an imperial concubine; "ash" may refer to the faded color of fallen petals. So this line can be interpreted in two ways: since the red is gone, the plum-blossom, now pale and gray, gives out only ashen fragrance; or more positively, it may mean that although the red is gone and the plum-blossom has become pale as ash, it still emits fragrance: a woman, although old, is still charming. If my conjecture is correct, the plum-blossom here might allude to a discarded favorite of Emperor Hsüan-tsung (*regnet* 712–756), Imperial Consort Plum-blossom (Mei Fei). She was given such a name by the emperor because of her great fondness for this flower but when Yang Kuei-fei became the new imperial favorite, Mei Fei was discarded and forced to move to the Shang-yang Palace. Whoever she may be, the woman in the poem lives alone in a palace.

The next two lines, I think, are not so much a direct description of the decayed palace as an indirect delineation of the woman's state of mind. For ten years she has been conscious of the painted beams being eaten by worms just as she has felt something gnawing at her own heart. As a hungry worm would not eat but sits there pushing yellow crumbs, so this woman, hungry for love, sits alone, tediously counting the crumbs of her days. Thus the woman feels grief over her youth which is being wasted like spring flowers blooming in vain and autumn leaves yellowing by themselves without attracting anyone's notice. In her room, the hanging blinds are the same but the emperor visits her no more. Where, then, is the emperor? At the Hua-ch'ing hot springs, surrounded by white phoenixes! Hua-ch'ing, at the foot of Mount Li in Shensi, was a famous hot springs resort favored by Emperor Hsüan-tsung and his favorite Yang Kuei-fei. Its water does not smell sulphurous and people believed its warmth to be caused by a layer of arsenic stones at its bottom, because arsenic stones retain heat for a long time.

The image in the last two lines suggests, I believe, an imperial bathing scene: a bevy of nude beauties—white phoenixes, accompanying the emperor, the only man they are supposed to please. Although this interpretation may sound rather erotic, it is not without foundation. A female phoenix is usually mentioned together with a dragon in Chinese as a compound, *lung-feng*, which means man and woman. As a dragon stands for an emperor so does a phoenix stand for a queen or an imperial concubine. Judging from the theme of the poem, taking the phoenixes as imperial concubines is much more natural and relevant than taking them as "attendant officials."[60] Phoenixes may have different colors but here the poet explicitly indicates that they are white, suggesting their fair complexion. Since the Chinese language does not indicate the singular or plural number of a noun, whether the "phoenix" here should be understood as one or more is up to the reader's own imagination. Seen in this way, this poem describes a discarded imperial concubine's inmost yearnings for love or her being carried away by repressed sexual desire, and her jealous conjectures as to the current amorous activities of her absent lord.

Song: Hard to Forget

Your house is truly easy to know—
     easy to know, yet hard to forget.
                                        —Ancient Verse

Along the narrow lane, facing gates open wide,
Delicate willows droop over painted halberds.
Screen shadows: bamboo patterns rise,
The flute sounds, blowing sun-color.
A bee speaks, circling the dressing mirror;
Moth-brows are brushed in imitation of Spring
     grass.
Clove knots promiscuously tied to twigs,
All over the railings, flowers face the evening.
                                        [p. 80]

The first two lines describe the appearance of an influential family's house. In my translation of the first line, I follow the traditional commentary, taking *chia-tao* to mean "a narrow lane" and taking *tung-men* as "gates facing each other." As a point of fact, in the past the gates of an influential family's residence opened on a quiet lane rather than a noisy thoroughfare. However, if we take *chia-tao* for a tree-bordered road, and *tung-men* for successive gates, then the first line can be translated as "a tree-lined road leads through successive gates." A road bordered with delicate willows run through gate after gate, following, in perspective, the picture of a deep cavern or tunnel opened by a road. This interpretation evokes a more picturesque and dynamic image, although it may be less historically accurate. In the T'ang dynasty, high officials above the third rank (the lowest being the ninth) lined the fronts of their houses on both sides of the road with painted halberds as dignified decorations. Now delicate willows droop over the painted halberds; as willows often symbolize women, this line seems also to suggest the image of women, fragile creatures, bowing to the halberds, symbols of dignity and power. How does a woman in such a family pass her days? She remains secluded in her lonely boudoir. A gentle breeze plays upon the bamboo screen, thus creating the flute-like sounds, and casting patterned shadows on the ground as the sun shines through it. The poet, however, achieves such visual and auditory effects in a more suggestive and complicated way: in literal translation, the screen's shadows make bamboo patterns; a flute's sound blows the color of the sun. The screen casts shadows because the setting sun shines obliquely on it. Moreover, it resembles in form a row of bamboo pipes banded together to make a *p'ai-hsiao,* a sort of Chinese panpipe—when the breeze blows on it and the sun tinges it with gold, one imagines that "the sound of flutes blows the color of the sun." This very successful image combines the visual and the auditory senses.

The room is so quiet that even the sound of the bamboo screen in the gentle breeze is audible. On such a quiet and lonely evening, the young woman dresses herself in front of a mirror; attracted by the fragrance of her cosmetics, a bee hums around her. The original verb *yü* also suggests that the bee is not really humming but speaking. A bee attracted by her fragrance, then, tries to speak to her or to beguile her with words of sympathy and indignation over her neglected love. Nevertheless, she paints on her eyebrows in imitation of Spring grass, dark, slender, and arched. As *ch'un-pi* (Spring emerald) may suggest distant mountains as well, her eyebrows may also look as dark as mountains in Spring or as beautifully arched as the outlines of the distant peaks. All her careful makeup is in vain, as the last two lines indicate. The seeds of cloves hide in their thick shells, which consist of two segments grown together; therefore, clove knots in Chinese literature symbolize the love of a man and a woman. In this poem cloves knot themselves together indiscriminately on the branches, suggesting the promiscuity of the man in this family, who takes liberties with many women. In contrast, all over the railings, flowers "face the evening": discarded concubines shrivel in their loneliness, their beauty displayed for no one's appreciation. As the title and the epigraph indicate, the poet probably went to visit a high official and met one of his concubines whom he could not forget and for whom this poem was written, either in sympathy with her loneliness or in order to express disapproval of the man's inconstancy.

Li Ho's sympathy for the neglected wife is typified further in another poem, "A Song of the Mansion by the River":

> In front of my house runs the river,
>   the way to Chiang-ling;
> The carp-wind rises, the lotus flowers grow old.
>
> At dawn, hairpins spur my hair to whiten; I
>   speak to the south wind:
> "It takes only one day to hoist the sail and
>   come back. . ."
>
> When crocodiles growled by the mouth of the
>   river and plum-rains fell,
> When wine-shops' streamers atop the poles were
>   changed to the green ramie,
> When surging waves were running white and
>   clouds were ruffled,
> I sent a powder-yellow oilcloth coat to my
>   lord and husband.
>
> The sound of wine in the new vats bitter and
>   powerless;
> The southern lake, a hectare of caltrop-blossom
>   white.
> Then before my eyes are a thousand miles
>   of sorrow,
> When Little Jade opens the screen, I see
>   the mountain colors.

[p. 126]

This poem describes a woman's emotions as she thinks of her husband away from home. She now dwells alone by the Yangtze River, and her husband is at Chiang-ling, a city on the north side of the upper course of the river, in modern Hopei province. In her yearning for her husband, the river in front of her house has no other significance than as the way to Chiang-ling. As the first line fixes the physical location, so the second line fixes the time. The carp-wind stands for the wind in the ninth lunar month, the autumn wind.[61] That lotus flowers are getting old in the autumn wind reminds her of the gradual loss of her youthful beauty. At dawn her hairpins urge her hair to turn white and at the same time urge her to arrange her coiffure. Yet, for whom does she arrange it? When this question comes to mind, she murmurs to herself, or rather, to the south wind, asking the wind to carry her words to her husband: it takes only one day to hoist the sail and come back. If he sets sail at dawn, by twilight he will be home. . . . The next four lines describe her long wait. The so-called plum-rains usually fall between the fourth and the fifth lunar months when plums are ripening, and bring a rainy season to the southern Yangtze River Valley. It was believed that crocodiles growled when it was going to rain, and during the rainy season, wine-shops' streamers (store signs usually made of cloth) would easily get wet, therefore they would be replaced by ones made of green ramie. It was on one such rainy day that she sent her husband an oilcloth coat for fear he would encounter rain on his way home. However, since then four or five months have passed and her husband has not returned. She brews wine, waiting for him to drink with her. But now in disappointment the dripping sound of the wine in the vat marks the passing time and only enhances her cheerless and disconsolate state. What can alleviate her sorrow? Turning her head to the lake in the south, she hopes that nature's beauty can distract her mind, but, on the contrary, a broad expanse of water, as white as a mirror, reflects only her face, pallid after eagerly waiting for so long.[62] Finally, when Little Jade, her maidservant, pushes open the screen and the mountain scenery painted on it greets the wife's eyes, her thoughts are fixed even more intently on her husband far beyond myriad peaks, and she then sees only sorrow, "a thousand miles long." Here the poet uses the striking image of great linear distance to evoke a sense of boundless sorrow. As a concrete poetic image, this figure evinces both the setting of the poem and the mood of the principal character whose thoughts, drawn forth by the illusion of the peaks on the decorative screen, rush to the husband a thousand miles away.

Undoubtedly, Li Ho's forte lies in the expression of women's inmost feelings. He professed to be the only "troubadour of love" in Ch'ang-an since the passing of the Han writer Ssu-ma Hsiang-ju in 117 B.C. Also equally a master of setting, he succeeds in evoking a sympathetic emotional response to his characters and empathetic sensory reactions to visual and auditory stimuli in their environments. In "Stone City at Dawn" his artistry is apparent.

Stone City at Dawn

The moon is setting over the Great Dike,
From the battlements roosting crows start up.
Fine dew moistens spheres of red;
Cold fragrance dissolves the night's drunkenness.

The Weaving Girl and the Cowherd cross the River of Heaven;
Willow mist fills the corners of the city wall.
The honored guest leaves his torn tassel;
Fading moth-brows duel with their paired green.

Spring curtains cling, net-like, silky as cicada wings.
Bedding embossed with faint gold flower-patterns.
"Before the curtains, catkins, light as crane feathers, whirl up.
To describe a vernal heart, there is nothing comparable."

[p. 95]

Located in today's Hupeh province (or according to some commentators, in present-day Nanking), Stone Wall is the native place of the famous Liang dynasty (502–556) courtesan, Mo Ch'ou, whose name means "Never Grieve." This poem describes Stone Wall at dawn, when the male guest is taking leave of the famous courtesan. The first four lines depict a calm and chilly spring morning when the moon is setting and roosting crows are beginning to wake. "Spheres of red" are red flowers, upon which fine dew has formed. The chilly fragrance of these flowers dispels the morning hangover brought about by the merry toasts of the night before. The next four lines describe the parting after a night of sensual pleasures. Like the Weaving Maid and the Cowherd (stars) who meet once a year across the River of Heaven, the man and the courtesan now part with each other at dawn as the mist mingles with the willows hanging over the corners of the city-wall. At this time, the courtesan's honored quest tears the tassel from his cap and gives it to her as a love token.[63] When she sees him off, she frowns in unhappiness and her eyebrows, conventionally described as "moth-brows," push together the two lines of green makeup which adorn them, as if they were dueling. Uncertain feelings continue to struggle in her inmost heart: "Does he really love me? Do I love him? Is this love or only carnal passion?" While these conflicting feelings struggle in her mind, she knits her brows. The last four lines express her loneliness after the quest's departure. The descriptions of her beautiful curtains and splendid bedding form a contrast to the emptiness of her heart in Spring, a feeling which cannot be compared more exactly than to the willow catkins floating in the air like crane feathers. A courtesan's heart is as light and uncontrollable as catkins drifting at the mercy of the wind.

Besides being a poet of love who is sensitive enough to penetrate the inmost regions of a woman's heart, Li Ho was also a man whose keen observer's eye could formulate artistic and objective descriptions of the beauties in front of him, as in "Song of a Beauty Combing Her Hair."

> Hsi Shih dreams at dawn, while raw-silk
>   curtains are cold;
> Her fragrant topknot and falling chignon half
>   scented by aloes and sandalwood.
>
> The windlass of the well turning with an
>   ee-ya! shriek of jade
> Wakes the lotus blossom by sleep newly satisfied.
>
> Twin phoenixes open her mirror to autumn-water
>   light;
> Undoing her topknot before the mirror, she
>   stands by the ivory bed.
>
> A tress of perfumed silk, a cloud, spreads over
>   the ground;
> Wherever the jade comb falls, an oil-smooth
>   gloss of hair.
>
> Again her delicate fingers coil the raven-colored;
> Blue-black, sleek, precious hairpins cannot
>   hold it.

Spring wind, dazzling, seductive, vexes the
   charmer's languor;
At eighteen, with hair so rich, she is overwhelmed.

Coiffure done, the beautiful chignon leans,
   but not askew.
In cloud-skirts she walks a few steps, a wild
   goose treading the sands.
Her back to people, in silence, where's she going?
Down the steps, she plucks herself a sprig of
   cherry blossom.

[pp. 132–133]

The first two lines depict the sleeping posture of the famous beauty Hsi Shih (fifth century B.C.).[64] She sleeps alone, her isolation suggested by the word "cold." Her falling chignon is fragrant by nature, only partly due to the perfumes she wears.[65] The next couplet describes her waking at dawn to the workday sounds of someone drawing water from a well, followed by another two-line description of her toilette. She opens the mirror's cover embroidered with twin phoenixes and undoes her tresses, standing beside the ivory bed. The word "standing" suggests that she is tall because her hair is long. When loosened, her perfumed tresses tumble to the floor, spreading out like a wisp of cloud. Since her hair is as soft as silk and as billowy as clouds, a jade-comb makes no sound in it. When she coils her raven hair again, it is so soft and sleek a precious hairpin cannot even stand up in it. With hair so rich, at so young an age, on a spring day so dazzling and seductive, she is overcome by the nameless longings of youth. The last four lines describe her graceful deportment after completing her morning ritual. As she moves, her skirt is as buoyant and fluffy as clouds and her manner is as gentle and refined as that of a wild goose treading on sand. She turns her back to people and, without uttering a word, she goes down the steps and plucks a sprig of cherry blossom in passing. This action is rich in symbolic meanings. Just as cherry blossoms in full bloom symbolize spring at its height, they also indicate the "spring feelings" of the young woman at the height of her beauty, dazzling with the bloom of youth, a frail flower to be admired (and plucked?) by the men around her. With the self-centered narcissism of youth, she plucks the flower, sensing its affinity with herself, in hopes she too will be loved as she loves the sprig of cherry blossom. Viewed from the standpoint of the first couplet, these last two lines can also be interpreted as reflecting her loneliness. Isolated from the people upon whom she has turned her back, she seeks the companionship of the flower, perhaps aware of the parallel to be found between its evanescent loveliness and her own, or perhaps simply to enhance her own charms.

This peom has received much praise. According to Fang Fu-nan, a Ch'ing dynasty commentator, "Among all the poems describing beautiful women, this one should be of the first rank."[66] Regarding the poetic theme, the same commentator remarks that "It describes the spring sorrows of a woman in her lonely boudoir. *Ying-t'ao-hua* (cherry blossoms), these three characters at the very end punctuate the mood of the entire poem. Not flowers in general but cherry blossoms in particular, it suggests that beautiful Spring has come to an end. Her secluded boudoir remains quiet, lonely and how lovelorn she is!"[67] Yao Wen-hsieh, another Ch'ing dynasty commentator, writes appreciatively, "Its remarkable words, rich and amorous; its description, exhaustive in detail;" and states that "her charming image preens and seems vividly visible."[68]

V *Descriptive Poems*

Although his finest aesthetic appreciations were written in praise of women, Li Ho's poetic sensibilities were also attuned to the beauty of the world at large. One may observe through his eyes the textures and movements of nature. In his poetic mind, these features are transformed into visions of beauty, which in its concrete and abstract forms is the subject of still other poems. Here a winter scene on the Yellow River is the topic.

Cold in the North

One side black reflects three sides purple;
The Yellow River icebound, fish and dragons die.
Three-foot thick treebark snaps against the grain;
Hundred-picul-weight carriages go out on the river water.

Frost-blossoms on the grass are big as coins;
A brandished blade cannot thrust into the maze of hazy sky.
Warring, whirling sea waters, flying icefloes roaring.
Mountain waterfalls soundless, hanging rainbows of jade.

[pp. 116–117]

Objectively, this poem depicts the bitter cold of the north. In reflection of the north which is extremely cold and dark, the sky in the other three directions turns dark purple. The Yellow River has become so icebound that its fish and dragons have frozen to death. Patterned bark, although three feet thick, breaks against the grain under the cold, and large carriages, although one hundred piculs in weight, pass safely across the river, the thickness and hardness of the ice indicating that it is mid-winter. In the wilds a stretch of grass is covered with frost-blossoms as big as coins. The sky itself is so hazy that even the air seems frozen; no matter how vigorously one brandishes his blade, it appears unable to cut into the foggy maze, either because the frosty air is so thick or because the person has become so stiff with cold that he cannot move quickly. In the sea, swirling ice-drifts crush and splash noisily, while on the mountain, waterfalls are frozen into rainbows of jade, hanging still and white. Each line employs a striking, concrete, and somewhat exaggerated image which juxtaposed with still other images, creates a collage of images of a single scene viewed from different angles.

Even in common hempcloth one may find beauty and aesthetic experience as well as a wealth of mythological allusions.

A Canto: Given a Piece of Hemp Cloth
by the Hermit in Lo-fu Mountains

Clinging, well-woven, the sky in the rainy river;
In the rain, in July, the Orchid-Terrace breeze.
The ancient immortal of Lo-fu often comes out of his cave;
On the thousand-year-old-stone bench, devil weavers cry.

Serpents' venom thick-exhaled: the cave's halls are dank.
River fish will not eat, stand with sand in their mouths.
I want to cut a foot of the sky inside the chest;
Maiden of Wu, don't say that your Wu scissors are blunt.

[pp. 57–58]

This is a descriptive poem about the fine, thin, and soft hemp cloth given to the poet by a hermit in the Lo-fu Mountains (in modern Kwangtung province). The first two lines contain a marvelous poetic image misunderstood by many commentators. In my opinion, they describe the fine quality of the hemp cloth and the coolness of wearing it in summer. This piece of hemp cloth is com-

pared to the sky reflected in a river in the rain. In this way, the cloth
is seemingly woven of rain, so fine are its yarns; it waves gently like
the water in the river, and in appearance it is as clear and clean as
the reflected sky. These images also suggest the comfort of wearing
the cloth: on hot July days one feels as refreshed as if one were
standing in the rain or in the breeze of the Orchid Terrace.[69] The
next couplet describes the fine workmanship of the hemp cloth. The
old immortal often comes out of the cave either to gather the *ko*
(Pueraria Thunbergiana) from which such fine cloth is woven or to
present the *ko* cloth to people. Whenever the immortal brings it out
of the cave, the devil weavers cry. Why? One possible reason is, as
Wang Ch'i has pointed out, that they begrudge the immortal giving
such a cloth so laboriously made to mortal men.[70] Another reason is
probably because a secret of nature is being divulged to human
beings, in the same sense as they cried when Chinese characters
were first invented by Ts'ang Chieh.[71] Suzuki suggests that they cry
because they are struck with wonder at the ancient immortal's
workmanship.[72]

The second stanza describes the hot weather of summer and the
poet's wish to have a dress made of such fine, cool hemp cloth. It is
so hot that serpents gasp and exhale thick venom in damp caverns,
and fish lose their appetites and stand up with sand in their mouths:
a weird image characteristic of Li Ho's rich imagination. On such a
hot day, the poet wants to cut a foot of the "sky" which is kept in the
chest, namely, the *ko* hemp cloth of the first line, and asks his
maiden from Wu, a place famous for its silks and dressmakers, to
make him a suit of summer clothes. Since the hemp cloth is very
fine, thin, and soft, the maiden's scissors should be able to cut it
easily and she should not voice any complaint.[73]

Li Ho displays his poetic talent not only in the description of
concrete objects but also in the embodiment of abstract impressions. Here is one of his best works about music:

Song: Li P'ing on the *K'ung-hou* Harp

Wu silk, Shu paulownia wood, stretching high Autumn;
Sky white, congealed clouds crumbling, not floating;
The Ladies of the River Hsiang shedding tears on the bamboo,
  the White-silk Girl sorrowful:
Li P'ing playing the *k'ung-hou* harp in the capital of China.

Mount K'un-lun jade shatters, phoenixes scream,
Lotuses weep dew, fragrant orchids smile.
In front of the twelve city gates the cold light melts;
Twenty-three strings move the Purple Emperor.

Where the goddess Nü Wa with smelted stones mended the sky,
Stones break, and the sky astonished, induces the Autumn rains.
In dreams, entering the Mythic Mountains to teach
   the Mythic Sorceress;
Aged fish leap the waves, scraggy dragons dance.
Wu Kang, sleepless, leans on the cassia tree;
A trail of dew flies aslant, wets the shivering hare.

[p. 17]

Except for the first line describing the musical instrument and the fourth line introducing the musician, every line embodies the feelings stirred by the music. Li P'ing was the poet's contemporary, an accomplished player of the *k'ung-hou* instrument, similar to Western harps, with twenty-three strings. The *k'ung-hou* Li P'ing plays in the poem is strung with the best silk from Wu (Kiangsu) and constructed of the best paulownia wood from Shu (Szechwan). The music he plays moves not only goddesses but floating clouds as well. The clouds are so absorbed in listening to the music that they stop moving and become frozen like lumps of ice, eventually to collapse from the reverberating sounds of the music that attacks them like a continuous shower of arrows shot from the strings of the *k'ung-hou* instrument. The verb *"chang"* has two basic meanings: (1) to stretch a bow; (2) to stretch musical strings, i.e., to pluck. Here I think the poet uses the second meaning to imply the first: frozen clouds collapse as they are struck by the sounds shot from the strings. As the music changes tone, it becomes clear and shrill, like the sound of jade being crushed, or screaming phoenixes.

Mount K'un-lun in the west of China, a mountain mentioned in many Chinese mythological works, is also famous for producing the finest jade. As feminine beauty is often compared to jade, so is a talented literary man compared to jade from Mount K'un-lun. Now the jade is probably crushed due to the impact of the music: the heart of a beautiful woman or a poet is broken, as if struck by the music which is full of violent passions.

Phoenixes are auspicious mythical birds; it was believed that when they appeared, the world would be at peace. But here phoenixes scream, probably because it is on Mount K'un-lun where they often roam about that the jade is being shattered by the music. Not to mention the world, the auspicious birds themselves cannot live in peace. Thus the effects of the music are always either directly or indirectly contagious. The music moves the plants to tears, causing lotuses to weep dew or orchids to bloom with radiant smiles. Music can alter even a physical phenomenon—melting the cold light: an image joining together the tactile, visual, and auditory senses.

Besides changing the physical phenomena of this world, the music also moves the Purple Emperor, the Taoist Celestial Ruler. But how? When the music reaches Heaven and shakes apart the colorful stones which the goddess Nü Wa has used to repair the sky, all Heaven is shocked, but at that very moment, as the music softens and flows melodiously, the Purple Emperor is moved to tears that become the rains of autumn.

The music is so fantastic that the listener is infatuated and, in a dreamlike state, endowed with mysterious powers, enters the Mythic Mountains to teach the Mythic Sorceress who herself is an expert on the *k'ung-hou.* To extend the meaning of this line: the best works of art can not only infatuate the general audience but also illuminate the experts in that art; to appreciate a work of art one has to wholly surrender oneself to it, as in dreams. The Mythic Mountains probably refer to the three legendary mountains in the eastern sea where old fish and scraggy dragons, rejuvenated and vitalized by the music, leap and dance among the waves. Finally, the music played by Li P'ing makes Wu Kang,[74] the Chinese Sisyphus, forget the tedious and fatiguing labor to which he was condemned as sleeplessly he listens to the music until midnight when the dew begins to fall.

Examined from the structural point of view, a consistent temporal order or sequence is suggested by the poem: the frozen clouds in the sky indicate noon or afternoon, the cold sunlight in front of the palace gates indicates sunset, autumn rains fall at twilight, and the shivering hare gets wet at midnight. In terms of place, since Li P'ing plays in the capital, the poem is closely related to actual circumstances: city gates and the palace, where palace ladies and the emperor gather, and where one often finds such objects as lotus, orchids, jade, phoenixes, etc.

In this poem Li Ho's poetic diction is conspicuous for its use of words denoting hardness or solidity, such as *ning* (to congeal, or frozen), *shan* (mountain), *yü* (jade), *shih* (stone), and for words suggesting fluidity or liquidity, such as *liu* (to flow or float), *t'i* (to weep), *ch'i* (to sob or weep), *lu* (dew), *jung* (to melt), *lian* (to smelt), *yü* (rain), *po* (waves), *t'iao* (to leap), *wu* (to dance), and *fei* (to fly).[75] In its overall artistic effect, this poem resembles a River of Heaven seven characters in width, flowing through the dark sky of the reader's imagination: every character is like a starry gem glittering in the reader's vision, and at the same time every character is like a musical note reechoing in his ears the very melodies played by Li P'ing.

VI *Divine Spirits*

Finally, let us take a look at Li Ho's poems on divine spirits, which differ from those on ghosts in two significant ways: they bear no direct relation to the poet's sufferings, and they are written from the point of view of the poet as an imaginative observer.

Song of the Divine Strings

In the western hills the sun sets, the eastern
hills darken.
A whirlwind blows the horses along, the horses tread
on the clouds.
Painted stringed instruments and plain pipes
sound, now light, now intricate;
With a rustling of flowery skirts, she treads
the autumn dust.

Cassia leaves brush the wind, the cassia trees
drop seeds;
Blue raccoons weep blood, and shivering foxes die.
On the ancient wall is a colored dragon with
a gold appliquéd tail;
The Rain God rides it away, into an autumn pool
of water.
The hundred-year-old owl has become a tree demon;
A peal of laughter and emerald fire now rise
from its nest.

[p. 130]

This song is about ceremonies of worship or sacrifice accompanied by string music played to please the gods. After sunset, as the sky

darkens, a whirlwind rises and blows clouds on which horses tread: a
god descends on horseback from Heaven. Then, in front of a shrine,
a witch begins to play music and to dance in order to please the god
and offer up prayers for his help in dispelling evil spirits. In answer,
the god shows his supernatural power by conjuring up a strong wind
and blowing cassia leaves and seeds off their branches. Then the god
begins to expel evil demons and mischievous spirits. The Chinese
believed that when an animal survived far past its regular age, it
became an evil spirit. It was said that a fox that lived a thousand
years became a sexually passionate woman, and one that lived a
hundred years became a beauty. Now, as the god begins to oust all
the evil spirits, blue racoons weep blood and shivering foxes die. As
for the dragon painted on the ancient wall of the shrine, a large spirit
which sometimes comes out to cause trouble, the god orders the
Rain God to ride it away into deep water. What remains is the worst
monster, a hundred-year-old owl that has become an arboreal demon and lives in an ancient tree by the shrine. The god starts a blue
fire in its nest and it immediately rises up with a peal of revolting
laughter: a show of scorn, because the old owl is also confident in its
own supernatural powers. Some commentators take the laughter in
the last line as the sound of fire and thus miss the owl's spiteful and
unyielding spirit, which is suggested by its eerie laughter.[76]
  The following is a similar poetic account of gods:

Divine Strings

The witch pours a libation of wine; clouds fill the sky.
A jade stove, a charcoal fire; incense tomtoms.[77]
Sea gods and mountain goblins come to sit in;
Paper money crepitates, whistling, whirling wind.

Love-longing wood, appliquéd golden dancing phoenixes;
Knitting her brows, she mumbles a charm, then plays a passage,
Calling stars, summoning spirits to accept offerings
    in goblets and dishes;
When mountain demons eat, men fall hushed and shaken.
Chung-nan sun's colors are low over the level cove.
Ah, God!—always exists between being and non-being.
Gods displeased, gods delighted, the evocatrix changes color,
Sending off the gods with ten thousand riders
    back to the green mountains.

                                                    [pp. 131–132]

This is a song inviting gods to come and enjoy sacrificial offerings. As the witch pours out a libation of wine in invitation, they come riding the clouds in such numbers that they darken the sky. The incense, ignited with a charcoal fire in a jade stove, puffs with the sound of a drum: a synaesthetic image of the auditory and olfactory senses, but I feel that it has a visual effect also. The smoke whirls up one ring after another, as if each ring of smoke comes out following the beat of a tomtom. As a whirling wind rises, paper money burnt for the use of the spirits or gods crackles and all gods and goblins come to take their places. Then, with a lute of "love-longing wood" (*Abrus precatorius*) adorned with dancing phoenixes, the sorceress, knitting her brows, mumbles an unintelligible charm and then demurely plays a tune. In this way, she calls down star spirits and summons goblins to accept the offerings laid out in goblets and on plates. When the mountain demons, although invisible, begin to eat, the pieces of food seem to break off and disappear as if they were being bitten, and the people, hushed and shuddering, watch in awe until the sun sinks westward into the valley. Whether or not there are gods is in the poet's mind an insoluble problem. He knows only the summoner changes her facial expression, supposedly according to whether the gods are delighted or displeased. Finally, she appears to send the gods, followed by their ten thousand ghostly riders, back to the green mountains.

Some commentators hold that Li Ho was a skeptic regarding the existence of gods, but here his skepticism is not unmixed with curiosity. His numerous poems whose subjects are various gods and sacrifices hold an excitement and intensity that is almost childlike. Beyond this, his images are so concrete and graphic that one senses the poet wavering somewhere between doubt and belief. Of one thing we may be certain, all supernatural phenomena held a particular fascination for Li Ho and his writing describes these in an uninvolved though animated fashion. Whatever his religious sentiment was in these matters, his interest in them was primarily as poetic subjects.

As I have shown above, Li Ho's poetic worlds are rich in diversity and deep in life experiences. He looked into his own heart and wrote, and therefore produced many poems concerning his personal sufferings. In most cases, however, his sufferings are objectified and transmuted into poetic emotion that can be shared by the reader, ancient or modern, Chinese and foreign. He also looked into other people's hearts and from this empathy wrote poems about other

people, society, history, beautiful women, and the supernatural. In
terms of profundity of experience, he explored many worlds that
had not previously been charted. For instance, his rancor against
the injustice of fate is that which after a thousand years becomes an
"emerald" in the earth; the sadness he experienced is what tugs at
his intestines until they become unnaturally straight; and human
emotions stirred by suffering, he found, is what makes even Heaven
grow old. In his poetic worlds, a palace girl wishes to go riding on a
fish slashing the waves; devil weavers cry on a thousand-year-old
stone bench and river fish stand up with sand in their mouths:
bizarre images present hitherto unexplored realms of experience. In
the perplexity of life, he asks: Who am I? Have my spirit and blood
truly come together? Touched deeply by the apparent heartlessness
of Time, he declares that even immortals in Heaven have died
countless deaths. In criticizing human desire that knows no bounds,
he concludes that even nature's fecundity fails to meet a magistrate's
greed. All this points to the fact that Li Ho probed human nature
and human life with deep insight. The breadth of his poetic worlds
includes not only his own personal experiences but also those of
society; they are not only of this world but also of worlds beyond and
worlds above, not only of men but also of ghosts and gods; they are
not only realistic but also surrealistic. Well said are Tu Mu's comments on Li Ho's poetry:

The continuous softness of misty clouds is insufficient to describe its manner; the distant stretch of water is insufficient to describe its feelings; the
gloriousness of spring is insufficient to describe its geniality; the bright
limpidness of autumn is insufficient to describe its character; the mast of a
ship extended against the wind and horses at the battle-front are insufficient
to describe its valor; a coffin made of tile and a tripod carved with seal
scripts are insufficient to describe its antiquarianism; flowers in season and
beautiful women are insufficient to describe its charms; a ruined kingdom
and a crumbled palace, or an earthen mound overgrown with wild grass are
insufficient to describe its rancor, enmity, sadness and sorrow; a whale
yawning with its mouth open and a great tortoise leaping from the sea, or an
ox-demon and a snake-god are insufficient to describe its exaggeration,
absurdness, grotesqueness and fantasy.[78]

Although abstract and figurative, Tu Mu's comments at least
affirm that Li Ho's poems are many-faceted both in style and in
content. His poems constitute a crystal globe, which, with his poetic

mind as the heart, radiates the light and heat of his poetic worlds on all its surfaces. It is luminous, powered by the poet's mind. In the poetic sky of the T'ang dynasty, Li Ho's poetry sometimes glitters with a carefree combination of synaesthetic images that have puzzled many critics; sometimes it glimmers ghostlike in the wind and rain, making the blood run cold; sometimes it sparkles distantly like an eternal jewel against the darkness of the past; sometimes it glistens like morning dewdrops on the leaves, delicate and dazzling, pleasing to the aesthetic eye; and sometimes it reflects the realities of this earth, exposing life's seamy underside and casting a clear light on human ugliness and greed.

In short, Li Ho's worlds include both nocturnal and diurnal scenes; the former expressing the inner, often gloomy aspect of his mind, but the latter expressing his visions of the outer world, sometimes dreary, often glittering. Li Ho is certainly not a poet who, as Arai Ken asserts, shows no "interest in the outer world," and whose poems "are expressed as a contemplation of the inner world he has gazed upon";[79] nor is he a poet who, according to the same scholar, "keeps moulding the only thought in his mind . . . and the content of this thought is festering resentment; this simply cultivated evil attachment gradually propagates by itself and the poet keeps living only on it and only for it."[80]

CHAPTER 3

A Kaleidoscope of Imagery and Euphony: His Language

P OETRY is an exploration of different worlds and of the language used by the poet; however, the worlds and the language explored in a poem are in fact two interdependent aspects of the same thing, aspects which form a poetic whole.[1]

Li Ho's poetry is noteworthy not only for the sensitivity and imagination shown by the poet in his apprehension of worlds about and within but also for its craft, the skill of the poet in his manipulation of the language. A poem may be seen as the best words arranged in the best order. Since each word has both a particular sense and sound, a poem becomes a kaleidoscope rich in imagery and euphony. The choices made by the poet, of course, affect both the nature and form of his imagery and the musical qualities created by the sounds of the words (euphony), and consequently dictate the varied appearance of the kaleidoscope. In other words, verbal elements determine poetic style; appreciating style begins with understanding language. If we compare the poetic worlds formed in the reader's mind to moving pictures on a screen, both of which appear with a certain speed, then we may say that verbal analysis is like slow motion or stills which temporarily stop the action to enable us to observe detail more clearly and perhaps even detect a little of the behind-the-scenes activity.

As I have observed, the worlds explored in Li Ho's poetry are various and have accordingly been expressed in varying modes or styles, each utilizing a distinct vocabulary and unique structure. Among these modes, however, it is his "violent feeling of sadness" (*ai chi chih ssu*) that is most often emphasized by critics; and his obscure and difficult style (*hui se chih tiao*) that is most often judged

84

harshly;[2] for instance, the Ming dynasty commentator Li Tung-yang (1447–1516) states:

Li Ho's poetry, every word of which strives for immortality, is, as a matter of fact, too elaborately carved, and lacking a spontaneous and natural effect. After reading through a poem, one finds pillars' capitals carved in the shape of a mountain *(shan-chieh)* and joists decorated with painted duckweed *(tsao-cho)* but without beams *(tung-liang).*[3]

This elaborate, picturesque quality may be seen in the lines: "Small cypresses resemble tiered fans;/ Plump pines shoot out cinnabar rosin" (p. 100). Although the statement applies in this instance, Li Ho's diction varies so greatly from one poem to another that it is difficult to understand such a generalization.

Li Ho could also write in a simple, flowing mode: "In your garden, don't plant trees;/ To plant trees will bring four seasons of sorrow" (p. 77). When a lighter mood called for it, he could display a touch of lovely lightness: "Flower branches, grass tendrils open in the eyes./ Small whites, long reds: Yueh girls' cheeks" (p. 41).

At other times, also in contrast to his elaborate style of description, his poetry could be possessed of a torpid gloominess: "The aged scene sluggish and heavy, nothing startled or flying,/ Fallen reds, remnant calyxes scattered in the gloaming" (p. 31). Often his words have a personal, conversational tone: "Alone, I ride in a chicken-coop cart;/ I myself feel I lack *bon ton*" (p. 98). Or a simple archaism: "Brambles for whips,/ Tigers for horses./ Running round and round,/ Beneath the city-walls of Yeh" (p. 94).

Although each of these modes is unique and each poem a world unto itself, all may be analyzed from the point of view of the major elements which together constitute the formal structure of each poem and determine its distinctive character. These, as defined by Professor Liu, are diction, syntax, versification, imagery, symbolism, and allusion.[4]

I *Diction*

Diction bears a direct relation to the poetic worlds explored. In a world of sadness, words are tinged with gloom; in a world of satire, words are related to objects or events in social reality or history; in a world of amorous atmosphere, words suggestive of sensuous or sexual experience are used; in a world of the shades or a world of the heavens, words are concerned with ghostly or supernatural things. Examples are not difficult to find. In the poem entitled "A Grieved Heart" (p. 54), discussed in the second chapter, the mood is set by the use of such descriptive phrases as "white hair" *(po-fa)*, "fading glow" *(lo-chao)*, "sick bones" *(ping-ku)*, "ancient walls" *(ku-pi)*, and "hardened dust" *(ning-ch'en)*. The verbs used are equally expressive: "grieve" *(shang)*, "wail" *(t'i)*, and "choked" *(yeh-yeh)*, all indicating sadness and decline. In contrast, "Exhortation No. 1" (p. 68) which describes an encounter between common people and a government official, abounds in words grounding it in the world of mundane affairs. Thus one finds words like "magistrate" *(shih-chün)*, "wood slaves" *(mu-nu)*, "silkworms of Wu" *(Wu-ts'an)*, "silk reels" *(ssu-chü)*, and "yellow millet" *(huang-liang)*.

In "Song of a Beauty Combing Her Hair" (pp. 132–133), the poet sets a tone of elegant amorousness. He describes "the charmer's lanquor" *(chiao-yung)*, her "cloud skirts" *(yün-chü)* and "precious hairpins" *(pao-ch'ai)*. In a ghostly poem like "Exhortation No. 3" (p. 69), a pervading sense of gloom dominates word choice. Rain is "ghostly" *(kuei-yü)*, grass "empty" *(k'ung-ts'ao)*, and the path is "dim and dark" *(ti-mi)*. Similarly, in "Song of Divine Strings" (p. 130), the vocabulary is associated with the supernatural: "blue racoons" *(ch'ing-li)*, "shivering foxes" *(han-hu)*, "tree demons" *(mu-mei)*, and "emerald fire" *(pi-huo)*.

A. *Sensory Diction*

Viewed from a different angle, Li Ho's diction reflects the sensory apprehensions of a sensuous man. Besides being an acute observer who missed little in his environment, he also experienced people and events directly through his senses. Flowers and grasses reached out and touched him with tendrils of fragrance and patterns of color; women were conglomerates of texture, scent, and motion; even the air itself stimulated his visual, auditory, olfactory, and tactile faculties. The world thus apprehended is wondrous in its endless variety, well beyond the power of an individual to control or even organize into comfortable patterns easily understood by the rational mind. As Lu Yu (1125–1210), a Sung dynasty poet, put it: "Li Ho's words are like raiment of one hundred patches, multicolored and dazzling to the eye, which no one can steadily gaze upon."[5] Another perspective may be gained by examining Li Ho's language from the viewpoint of individual senses.

B. *Visual Words*

Visually, Li Ho's poetic language is some of the richest in the history of Chinese literature. In comparison with several other T'ang poets, notably Han Yü, Wang Wei (701–761), and Meng Chiao (751–814), the Japanese scholar Kamio Ryūsuke concludes that color words in Li Ho's poetry are at least twice or perhaps four times as rich,[6] and Li Ho uses light words twice as frequently as the other poets.[7] Thus, Kamio supports Lu Yu's impressions of the dazzling variegation of Li Ho's poetry.

According to Arai Ken's statistics, among the 15,517 words in the poetry of Li Ho, there are 513 color words, accounting for 3.3 percent of the total.[8] A breakdown of these figures is as follows:

White	Green	Red	Blue	Gold	Yellow	Silver
113	88	85	78	73	22	21
Purple	Black					
20	13					

In addition to color words, according to Kamio Ryūsuke's statistics, among the 15,993 words in Li Ho's poetry (note the disparity with Arai Ken's total), there are 230 light words, accounting for 1.4 percent.[9] The details are:

Sun	Moon	Star	Brilliance	Ghost Fire	Lamp Light
40	68	28	67	7	17
Light of Miscellaneous Objects					
3					

The color of light for Li Ho is white; therefore, he often uses white to describe his impressions of a field in the sun or autumn which is traditionally associated with white. For example, "The autumn wilds bright, the autumn winds white," (p. 56) or "Autumn white, distant, distant sky,/ The sun fills the road before my gate" (p. 77).

Often a color word is used as metynomy, and is modified by a sensory or emotive adjective. In other words, Li Ho's response toward color shows itself not simply through visual perception, but often through the other senses. For example, he uses red *(hung)* to stand for a red flower, and has grasped such red sensuously as "cold red" *(leng-hung)*, "old red" *(lao-hung)*, "sorrowing red" *(ch'ou-*

hung), or "failing red" *(shuai-hung)*. Highly sensitive to color, Li Ho seems to have favored a moist green that glimmers in the distance, as in the lines: "Dark fireflies fill the Liang Palace" (p. 18), or "A cold emerald candle" (p. 27).

Regarding the use of color words, several observations may be made. The most frequently used colors are white, green, and red. Often they are used together in contrast to one another. Either green against white ("One night green bracts greet the white dawn") (p. 91), white against red ("Autumn white, fresh reds die") (p. 133), or red against green ("Nine Peaks quiet and green tearful flowers red") (p. 40).

By their archetypal significance and many cultural associations, colors can express a person's inmost feelings without further reliance on words. Used by an artist such as Li Ho, they can create an instant empathy between creator and those who observe his creation. According to the newly emerging science of functional psychology, color preference highlights significant aspects of personality.[10]

In Chinese culture, white is the color of earth and the west, said to influence the lungs and small intestines.[11] It is also symbolic of sorrow. In general, it signifies innocence, hope, purity, perfection, as well as winter, death, and the light of day. Emanuel Swedenborg, the Swedish philosopher, felt white to be light minus warmth, love unfelt.[12] The psychologist Max Lüscher calls a preference for white a "Yes" as opposed to the "No" of black, negation, and extinction. It represents a beginning, the blank page upon which no story has been written. A marked preference for such a color indicates a desire for release, and hope for happiness and/or perfection and always movement forward toward the future.[13] For Li Ho, white seems to have had all these meanings at one time or another: white variously describes the horse of a young knight errant, the purity and simplicity of undyed cloth wafted aloft, the clouds, and the chilly light of the autumn sun.

As a universal symbol, green signifies spring, new life, hope, the breaking of shackles. In the Chinese *Classic of Changes (I Ching)*, it signifies the sprout overcoming obstacles in its upward movement toward light and life.[14] To the functional psychologist, green corresponds to the mighty sequoia towering over lesser trees in the forest, a sense of superiority and pride; hence, also tension from worry over possible loss of standing or personal failure.[15] One is reminded of Li Ho's pride in his royal lineage: "This horse is no common horse./ It is the very spirit of the Equine Stars" (p. 47), and of his sense of dejection and failure when "at twenty he did not gain the day" (p. 92).

The spirit of red is action, desire, anger, love, martyrdom.[16] In Chinese folklore it is the fiery color of the south, governing the heart and intestines.[17] As a pure color, gazed upon, it speeds up the pulse, raises the blood pressure, and increases respiration. Lüscher observes that red is "the urge to achieve results, to win success, to hungrily desire all those things which offer intensity of living and fullness of experience, all forms of appetite and craving."[18] This impulse toward activity and success appears in Li Ho's works in the form of his exuberant pursuit of position and recognition in Ch'ang-an: "I have a sword that bids adieu to my homeland,/ Its jade edge can cut the clouds./ A champion gallops his horse to Hsiang-yang,/ His very spirit bearing the Spring" (p. 40). The sensuous qualities of his writings, the vein of eroticism, and the richness of his imagery are equally expressive of the vitality and impulse toward experience characterized by a preference for red, perhaps compensating for feelings of emptiness at his failure to gain official recognition.

C. Auditory Words

It has often been pointed out that *t'i* (cry) and *ch'i* (weep) are two of Li Ho's favorite words.[19] In his poetry, not only birds, crows, monkeys, mole-crickets, wild geese, and phoenixes cry, but also goddesses and ghosts, flowers and bronze camels. In Li Ho's ears, not only are there sounds of the zither, the water clock, singing, and crying, but also the sound of clouds: "On the silver shore, the floating clouds imitate the sound of water" (p. 35), or even the sound of the sun: "Hsi Ho strikes the sun, the sound of glass" (p. 38). His sensitive ear perceives even a "frozen sound"—quiet: "The stony brook of frozen waves sound" (p. 103).

Li Ho uses many onomatopoeic words, such as *lung-lung* (roaring), *ting-ting* (ding-a-ding), *tung-tung* (tomtom), *p'eng-p'eng* (bang, bang), *ling-lung* (tinkling), and *lang-tang* (clinking). Especially, Li Ho seems to have enjoyed the silvery sound of jade: "Treading on the mist and riding the wind, she returns,/ Her shaking jades heard on the mountain" (p. 123), and "The windlass on the well turning with an ee-ya! shriek of jade" (p. 132).

Extremely auditory is the effect of the following couplet: "Down flies a female mandarin duck,/ Water in the pond resounds—ker-plop! ker-plop!" (p. 128) The *k'ap-k'ap* (ker-plop! ker-plop!) sound describes the gentle, undulating lap of water suddenly disturbed by the duck flapping down. The effect of these two lines is similar to that of a well-known *haiku* by the Japanese poet Yosa Buson (1716–83): "Spring's sea—all day, all night, rise and fall, rise and fall . . ." (*Haru-no-umi hinemosu notari notari kana*).[20] *K'ap-k'ap* in Li Ho's line has an effect similar to that of *notari-notari* in the *haiku:* the rising and falling of light waves in a pond or on the sea in spring.

D.   *Olfactory, Gustatory, and Tactile Diction*

The most noticeable olfactory word is "fragrance" or "scent" (*hsiang*). Li Ho felt and described not only the fragrance of flowers, of hair, of lips, of silk curtains, of quilts, but also the subtle fragrances of rain, mist, and bamboo. Yang Shen (1488–1559), a scholar of the Ming dynasty, called attention to the lines: "I scrape off its green luster to inscribe the *Songs of the South*,/ Rich fragrance, vernal powder, line on line in black" (p. 64), and "Bamboo's fragrance fills the chilly quiet;/ The powdered joints painted fresh emerald" (p. 99). Yang Shen insisted that "Bamboos do have fragrance which one does not notice unless one smells them closely."[21]

Li Ho uses the word "*hsiang*" (fragrance) in the same way he uses color words, apprehending it in more than one sense: "flying fragrance" (*fei-hsiang*), "cold fragrance" (*han-hsiang*), "green fragrance" (*lü-hsiang*), and "piercing fragrance" (*tz'u-hsiang*). Further, Li Ho's poetry includes the names of a great variety of fragrances, such as "aloes" (*chen-hsiang*), "sandalwood" (*t'an-hsiang*), "cloves" (*ting-hsiang*), and "musk" (*she*).

Although his gustatory words are comparatively few, Li Ho uses the word "wine" (*chiu*) sixty times and describes numerous banquet and drinking settings. In addition, he in many places describes rare delicacies to tempt the palates of nobles and immortals: "tail of carp" (*li-yü-wei*) or "gibbons' lips" (*hsing-hsing-ch'un*). In another poem he speaks of "Catching phoenixes at Cinnabar Cave to fill one's own travelling kitchen,/ And macaques the size of a fist, cannot possibly be enough to eat" (p. 114).

In connection with the *tactile* sense, another characteristic of Li Ho's diction is the propensity for words with the quality of hardness. As Ch'ien Chung-shu, a modern scholar, remarks, Li Ho has this feature in common with F. Hebbels, Edgar Allan Poe, and Charles Baudelaire: all like to use hard substances like minerals and rocks in their metaphors or comparisons.[22] In Li Ho's poetry, nouns with a hard quality are, for example: "jade" *(yü)*, and objects of jade, "jade wheel" *(yü-lun)*, "jade bow" *(yü-kung)*, "jade plate" *(yü-p'an)*, "jade blade" *(yü-feng)*, and even "jade rainbow" *(yü-hung)*. In addition, he favored "glass" *(liu-li)*, "coral" *(shan-hu)*, "amber" *(hu-p'o)*, "stone" *(shih)*, "sword" *(chien)*, and "bones" *(ku)*. Metals are frequently mentioned: "gold" *(chin)*, "brass" or "bronze" *(t'ung)*, "silver" *(yin)*, "iron" *(tieh)*, and "lead" *(ch'ieh)*. Adjectives and verbs often amplify the highly tactile quality of his imagery. The poems often contain such hard verbs as "break" *(sui)*, "crush" *(ya)*, "rap" or "beat" *(ch'iao)*, "scrape" *(kua* or *hsüeh)*, etc.

Li Ho also uses tactile words to modify color words and thus create compounds such as "cold red" *(leng-hung)*, or "cold green" *(han-lü)*. His favorite words for expressing tactile experience are "cold" *(leng* or *han)*, "wet" *(shih)*, "warm" *(nuan)*, and "frozen" or "congealed" *(ning)*. He attributes coldness not only to water, wind, and dew, but also to "fragrance" *(han-hsiang)* and "cold light" *(leng-kuang)*. To him, not only is the sun warm but even the grass and clouds.

As a sensuous poet and sensuous man, Li Ho certainly had "the same essential quality of transforming an observation into a state of mind,"[23] as that which T. S. Eliot found in the Metaphysical Poets, for in him there was "a direct sensuous apprehension of thought or a re-creation of thought into feeling."[24] For example, the lonely desolation of a scene in late spring is apprehended through the senses: "The aged scene sluggish and heavy, nothing startled or flying,/ Fallen reds, remnant calyxes scattered in the gloaming" (p. 31). The grimness of the battlefield and the tragic resolution in soldiers' minds is expressed through sensory observation: "Half rolled, scarlet banners nearing the river Yi,/ Frost heavy, drums cold, the sound cannot rise" (p. 25). Here the image of the sound is synaesthetic, the dull thud of sticks on the cold drum head creates a sound so slow and deep that the poet says of it that it is unable to follow its nature which is dispersal, it "cannot rise."

E.   *Emotive Words*

Wang Ssu-jen (1575–?), in his preface to *Ch'ang-ku shih chieh* (Commentaries of Li Ho's Poems), points out that Li Ho has a liking for words like "ghost" *(kuei)*, "weeping" *(ch'i)*, "death" *(ssu)*, and "blood" *(hsüeh)*.[25] Each of these words is highly emotive, creating responses in the reader by associations, both personal and cultural.

In Chinese, certain words about nature have various associations, such as "cloud" *(yün)*—"sexual love," as in *yün-yü;* "wind" *(feng)*— "romantic feelings," as in *feng-ch'ing* or *feng-liu,* "amorous" as in *feng-sao* or "charm" as in *feng-yün;* "flower" *(hua)*—"beauty" or "beautiful," as in *hua-jung.*

In Li Ho's poetry in particular there are a number of fairly ordinary words which within the context suggest the supernatural. These include "mist" *(yen, yeh,* or *wu),* "vapor" *(cheng, fen-yün),* "dim and dark" *(ti-mi).* Other words in this vein are "dream" *(meng),* "demons" *(mei),* "lacquer torches" *(ch'i-chü).* In addition, he uses numerous words indicative of the creatures of the mythical worlds beyond the ordinary that call up emotions and associations both cultural and individual: "Blue Lion" *(ch'ing-ni),* "griffins" *(ya-yü),* "phoenixes" *(feng, feng-huang, or luan).*

Noticeably, in his numerous poems about women, Li Ho uses those words suggestive of intimacy or feminine beauty that occupy a conspicuous place in his diction, words such as: "bed" *(ch'uang),* "pillow" *(chen),* "silk" *(ssu),* "waist" *(yao),* "moth-brows" *(o-mei),* "clouds and rain" *(yün-yü).*

All his life Li Ho struggled with consumption, so he was very conscious of the decline of his own body; words related to this include "white hair" *(po-fa),* "sick bones" *(ping-ku),* "muscles cold and thin" *(chi-leng* or *shou),* all eliciting an empathetic response from the reader.

When Seto Yasuo comments on a certain poem that the poet appears to be "trying to cram it with all the impressions he can,"[26] he could be speaking about almost any poem by Li Ho, for each is filled from beginning to end with rich words full of meanings and associations which stimulate both the reader's mind and his senses.

II Syntax

The syntax of Chinese poetry is different from that of classical Chinese poetry mainly in the following respects: 1) Words in poetry enjoy a higher degree of fluidity as parts of speech than in prose. 2) The word order of poetic language often differs from that of prose, and may involve inversions. A common pattern of syntax in prose is

Subject + Verb + Object; adjectives and adverbs normally precede the nouns and the verbs they modify. In poetry, the order is often reversed. 3) In poetry, particles and sometimes verbs that can be understood are often omitted. The syntax of Li Ho's poetry can also be observed in these three different aspects.

A. *Fluidity*

Parts of speech in Li Ho's verse enjoy a protean fluidity, thus lending his lines a dynamism and ambiguity which contribute to the legend of his being both eccentric and mysterious. By means of repetition a verb or noun takes on an adverbial function. Examples of the former are to be found in: "The sun's setting rays, faint light, sprinkling red" *(Jih-chiao tan-kuang hung sa-sa)* (p. 34); "From the sky brokenly drops the pure jade fragrance" *(Po-t'ien sui-sui to ch'iung-fang)* (p. 34). Here the verbs *sa* ("sprinkle") and *sui* ("shatter") are repeated, a device itself unusual, and positioned in such a way in the line as to modify an adjective and a verb.

Li Ho sometimes simply repeats the same verb to create a line more dynamic in rhythm as well as in meaning without altering its function as a verb. For example: "Go, go to run the hounds and return;/ Come, come to sit and cook a lamb." *(Ch'ü-ch'ü tsou ch'üan kuei/ Lai-lai tso p'eng kao)* (p. 143). Here the reduplication of the verbs "go, go" and "come, come" have the effect of short trumpet blasts sending hunters off into the fields and summoning them back.

In another instance of repetition in the line "Dew flowers fly and fly; carelessly the wind blows the grass" *(Lu-hua fei-fei feng ts'ao-ts'ao)* (p. 33), a noun acquires additional meaning from the repetition and its syntactical usage as an adverb. *Ts'ao-ts'ao* as a compound usually means "hastily" or "perfunctorily." Just as droplets of dew fly down, so the wind blows swiftly and carelessly. However, since *ts'ao* as a noun means "grass," *feng ts'ao-ts'ao* could also suggest that the wind blows carelessly over the grass.

In a number of cases nouns are used as verbs. The syntax of a line like *Pu ch'ien hua-ch'ung fen k'ung tu* (Don't let silverfish moth them to powdery nothingness) (p. 37), for instance, is somewhat ambiguous. *Tu* usually acts as a noun meaning "a book or cloth-eating insect," but here it seems to be used as a verb meaning "to nibble" or "to eat as a moth," being modified by *fen* (powder) and *k'ung* (nothingness).

B. *Inversion and Omission*

As previously mentioned, alteration of regular word order is a
common device in Chinese poetry. Inversions justify themselves on
the grounds that they heighten certain effects in rhyming, antithetical structure, and emphasis. In lines like "The dust by song stirred
on wormy beams lies;/ Dancing silk festoons like long clouds are"
(*Ko ch'en tu-mu tsai/ Wu ts'ai ch'ang-yün ssu*) (p. 101), the verbs
(*tsai* and *ssu*, "lie" and "resemble") come after the objects (*tu-mu*
and *ch'ang-yün*, "wormy beam" and "long clouds") because the two
lines have the same syntactic structure and *ssu*, a rhyme word, must
be at the end of the line.

Inversions of subjects and predicates can be found in the following example: *Ching shih chui yüan ai/ Chu yün ch'ou pan ling*
(Startled at rocks falling, apes wail;/ Bamboo clouds look sorrowful:
half peaks) (p. 26). In the first line, the subject *yüan* (apes) comes
after the predicate "startled at rocks falling." The placement of the
verb *ching* (startle) at the beginning of the line has somewhat the
effect of startling the reader. In the second line, the subject is *pan
ling* (half peaks) and the predicate that comes before it is *chu yün
ch'ou* (Bamboo clouds look sorrowful). In normal word order, these
two lines should read: *Yüan ai ching shih chui/ Pan ling chu yün
ch'ou* (Apes, startled at falling rocks, wail;/ At half peaks, clouds
growing on bamboo look sorrowful).

Sometimes word order is changed simply for rhetorical effect. In
the line *Hen ch'ang hua jung hsieh* (When singing resentfully, my
youthful face is consumed) (p. 105), *hen ch'ang* is simply a
euphemistic expression of *ch'ang hen;* the former which takes *hen* as
an adverb to modify *ch'ang* (to sing resentfully) sounds more indirect than the latter which takes *hen* as an object of *ch'ang* (to sing
resentments).

Parataxis, especially parataxis of nouns, occurs very often in
classical Chinese poetry, due partly to the absence of inflections in
the language and to the formal restriction of the poetic line to five or
seven syllables. Juxtaposition of nouns can have prompt, visual effects in the description of an object or scene. No verbs or particles
are used, but nouns with adjectives are juxtaposed, leaving the
action of the poem as well as grammatical and semantical relations
for readers to fill out: "Spring willows, southern path, posture;/ Cold
flowers, chilly dew, poise" (p. 89).

Sometimes in a couplet the first half of each line contains a verb while the second half consists of a noun phrase, the syntactic relation between the two halves being left unexplained: "Butterflies rest on China pinks—hinges of silver;/ Water congeals into duck-head green—coins of glass" (p. 55).

C. *Negation of Kinetic Verbs and Non-antithesis*

Li Ho often uses a negative adverb before a kinetic verb and thus creates in his poetry a particular effect of "kinetic stasis." The negative adverbs most often used are *pu* and *wei*, for example: *Lien-tai p'ing-p'u ch'ui pu ch'i/ Shuang chung ku han sheng pu ch'i* (The sword is like a white silk sash lying flat, cannot be blown aloft./ Frost heavy, drums cold, the sound cannot rise) (p. 25). Here the adverb *pu* modifies the verb *ch'i*, producing the idea that the sword is actually supple cloth frozen in eternal tension, unable to rise. In line two, this verb-adverb combination suggests the slow rumbling of sound trapped like a layer of fog next to the ground, too heavy to follow its own nature which is to radiate in all directions.

Sometimes the adjective *wu* is used in the same way to modify a movement-oriented noun (in translation equivalent to a gerund or a noun modified by a participle in English grammar). For example, *Lao-ching ch'en-chung wu ching-fei/ Ti wu ching-yen hai ch'ien-li* (The aged scene sluggish and heavy, nothing startled or flying./ On the earth no startled smoke; the sea a thousand miles) (p. 31).

On the other hand, Li Ho shows a very strong antipathy toward the use of antithesis. Not one of his two hundred and forty-two poems uses the seven-syllable Regulated Verse form so popular in his time. As Wang Li-hsi has pointed out, among Li Ho's forty-six poems in the *yüeh-fu* style collected by Kuo Mao-ch'ien (fl. 1264–1269) and included in his *Anthology of Yüeh-fu Poems (Yüeh-fu Shih-chi)*, only ten poems have antithetical couplets of which very few have observed perfectly the rules governing the form.[27]

Traditionally, the middle couplets ("antithetical couplets") of Regulated Verse are rigidly governed by rules which prescribe that they must contrast with one another in sense as well as in sound and also observe the following: 1) Each syllable in the first line should contrast in tone with the corresponding syllable in the next line. 2) Each syllable should be of the same grammatical category: noun against noun, verb against verb, adjective against adjective, etc. 3) The words which contrast with each other should refer to the same category of things: color against color, flower against flower, animal against animal, etc.

The effect created in these couplets tends to be "imagistic" which, as defined by Kao Yu-kung and Mei Tsu-lin,[28] makes them descriptive as opposed to assertive, composed of fragmentary images (usually nouns or noun phrases), discontinuous in rhythm, possessed of a static quality conducive to visualization and reflection, and lacking in an overall organization—effects also found in many of Li Ho's lines, though not antithetical couplets. The following line typically illustrates these qualities: "Cavalry maidservants, yellow bronze, chain-linked armor;/ Silken banners, perfumed staves, gold-painted leaves" (p. 56). While there is an implied spatial relationship here, there is no syntactical relation. The images are organized into short, static units that cause the reader to pause and contemplate the scene thus described.

In "propositional" lines, the syntactical rhythm urges one on, from line to line following the musical flow, as in:

> I will cut off the dragons' feet, chew the dragons' flesh,
> So that they can't turn back in the morning or lie down at night;
> Left to themselves the old won't die, the young won't cry.
>
> [p. 96]

Thus, one is able to observe a syntactical and logical relationship among the clauses and phrases, some of which modify or logically lead to one another, instead of merely stating or implying a spatial connection between isolated images. "Propositional" lines, rather than simply objectively describing an object or scene, tend to be subjective and assertive, calling not so much for visualization on the part of the reader as judgment. In fact, as a result of non-antithetical, non-imagistic language, most of Li Ho's lines are much more varied and flexible than those by poets who follow the more rigid formats or who choose to express themselves in a slower, more static imagistic manner. The following poem is a good example:

Bitter Bamboos: A T'iao-hsiao Ballad

> Allow me to speak of the time when
>   Hsüan-yüan reigned,
> Ling-lun gathered bamboos, twenty-four in all.

> Ling-lun gathered them from Mount K'un-lun;
> Hsüan-yüan issued an edict to divide them
> equally into twelves.
> Ling-lun used them to standardize the musical scale;
> Hsüan-yüan used them to modulate the Primeval
> Breaths.
> At that time when the Yellow Emperor ascended
> to Heaven,
> All twenty-three pipes went along with him,
> Leaving only one pipe to be played in the
> human world.
> Without virtue one cannot obtain this pipe;
> This pipe lies buried in the Shrine of Shun.

[pp. 108-109]

In this poem the poet recounts the story of the only pitch-pipe left in the world at the Shrine of Shun, the legendary emperor of Confucian virtue. The pipe made of bamboo is "bitter" because it, like virtue, has been sorely neglected, suggesting that the reign itself lacks virtue or its virtuous influence cannot prevail. In the poem, the language is "propositional" rather than "imagistic" in Kao and Mei's terms, and its rhythm is continuous. This fluidity is enhanced by the repeated use of words like *ts'ai* (gather), *i-chih* (with which), *Ling-lun*, *Hsüan-yüan*, and *kuan* (pipe). The syntax is scarcely different from classical Chinese prose, but among its regular seven-syllable lines is an unusual exception: a nine-syllable fourth line. The two additional beats come at the beginning of the line; therefore, rather than interrupting the rhythmic flow of the seven-syllables in the previous lines, it instead charges the prevailing rhythm to flow forward with even greater impetus. Even more so when the two syllables added (Hsüan-yüan) are a repetition of the same sounds that occur in the first line. Thus, with words and sentence patterns repeated so many times, the rhythm becomes steadily more fluid.

Syntactically speaking, Li Ho's lines tend to be more propositional than imagistic, more fluent than discontinuous. The obscurity of his poetry does not lie so much in the diction or the syntax as in the peculiarities of the poet's imagination and sensibility. I shall discuss these points in terms of imagery later on.

III *Versification*

The two verse forms most commonly used by T'ang poets are Ancient Verse (*Ku-shih*) and Regulated Verse (*Lü-shih*). The former, also called Ancient Style (*Ku-t'i*), has no fixed length or tone pattern, and permits changes of rhymes in one poem; the latter, which is the main form of the Modern Style (*Chin-t'i*), confines each poem to eight lines, has a prescribed tone pattern, and requires the use of the same rhyme throughout the poem and two antithetical couplets in the middle. Besides these forms, there are two others which are regarded as subdivisions of Modern Style Verse: the Quatrain (*Chüeh-chü*), which metrically corresponds to half of an eight-line Regulated Verse, and Multiple Verse (*P'ai-lü*), in which antithetical couplets between the opening and concluding couplets can be extended to an indefinite number rather than the two in Regulated Verse.[29]

Each of the above verse forms comprises two types: the five-syllable and the seven-syllable. According to verse forms, Li Ho's two hundred and forty-two poems can be classified and compared with those of a later T'ang poet, Li Shang-yin,[30] as follows:

	Li Ho	Li Shang-yin
Five-syllable Ancient Verse	67 (27.6%)	29 (4.9%)
Seven-syllable Ancient Verse	66 (27.6%)	18 (3.0%)
Five-syllable Regulated Verse	12 (4.8%)	146 (24.5%)
Seven-syllable Regulated Verse	0 (0%)	120 (20%)
Five-syllable Quatrain	31 (12.7%)	32 (5.4%)
Seven-syllable Quatrain	22 (9%)	201 (33.5%)
Five-syllable Multiple	7 (2.7%)	52 (8.7%)
Regulated Verse		
Three-syllable Ancient Verse	2 (0.8%)	0
Four-syllable Ancient Verse	1 (0.4%)	0
Mixed Style	35 (14.4%)	0
Total Number	242 (100%)	598 (100%)

On the basis of the above chart the following points may be made:
1) While Li Shang-yin's favorite verse form is Regulated Verse, Li Ho much prefers Ancient Verse. More than half of Li Ho's poems are Ancient Verse, either five-syllable or seven-syllable, while the seven-syllable Regulated Verse that was flourishing at the time was completely ignored by Li Ho.

2) Li Ho's thirty-one five-syllable Quatrains and twenty-two seven-syllable Quatrains contain very few antithetical couplets. Even though he has seven poems in the Multiple Regulated Verse form, three of them are relatively short, each with only twelve lines containing four antithetical couplets; the longest one of one hundred lines should be regarded as an exception. Obviously Li Ho's poetry shows a strong tendency against the use of antithesis.

3) In addition to poems in five and seven-syllable lines, Li Ho has one in four-syllable and two in three-syllable lines. More remarkably, Li Ho has as many as thirty-five poems in lines of varied length, ranging from three to nine syllables (Mixed Style). Lines with irregular numbers of syllables are completely lacking in Li Shang-yin's poetry.

As I have indicated, Regulated Verse is a very strict form with fixed length and prescribed tone patterns, while Ancient Verse does not have any fixed rules: lines continue as long as one pleases, and rhyme changes are permitted as often as necessary. Apparently, Ancient Verse was much more suited to Li Ho's poetic temperament. Wang Shih-chen (1526–1590), a Ming critic, remarked that "Li Ch'ang-chi follows his own mind's instruction; therefore, his poems sometimes sound strange. Moreover, he also has lines that take people by surprise."[31]

Furthermore, the sound and the sense of a poem are inseparable. Syntactical rhythm is often influenced by the verse form, just as metrical rhythm is often modified by snytax. Although the basic metrical rhythm of a five-syllable line is X X/X X X (each X represents a syllable, irrespective of tone) with a pause after the second syllable, it is often modified because of syntactical necessity. In Li Ho's poems we find several variations as follows:

a) X X/ X / X / X
   ping-ku / tu / neng / tsai
   (Sick bones / alone / can / exist) (p. 19)
b) X / X / X X / X
   shen / yü / t'ang-p'u / wan
   (Body / with / pond rushes / twilightens) (p. 18)
c) X / X / X / XX
   chih / k'o / ch'eng / hsianghan
   (Woven / it can / receive / fragrant perspiration) (p. 19)

d) X X / X X / X
   an-shang / *hu-tieh* / *fei*
   (On the bank / butterflies / fly) (p. 24)
e) XX / X / XX
   ch'un-feng / *ch'ui* / *pin-ying*
   (Spring breezes / blow / sidelocks' shadows) (p. 23)

Again, the basic metrical rhythm of a seven-syllable line is
X X/X X/X X X with two minor pauses after the second and the
fourth syllables. In Li Ho's poetry, however, one finds many variations:

a) X X / X X / X / X / X
   k'ung-po / *ning-yün* / *t'ui* / *pu* / *liu*
   (Sky white / congealed clouds / crumbling / not / floating.) (p. 17)
b) X X / X X / X X / X
   Chin-chia / *hsiang-lung* / *ch'ien-lun* / *ming*
   (Golden house / fragrant street / a thousand wheels / rumble)
   (p. 29)
c) X X X / X / X / X / X
   i-nan-ts'ao / *sheng* / *lan* / *hsiao* / *jen*
   (Son-getting herb / grows / orchids / smile at / people) (p. 30)
d) X X / X / X / X X / X
   chiu-k'e / *pei* / *han* / *Nan-shan* / *ssu*
   (Drinkers' / backs / cold / South Mountain / dies) (p. 30)
e) X X X X / X / X X
   shih-erh-men-ch'ien / *jung* / *leng-kuang*
   (In front of the twelve city gates / melts / cold light) (p. 17)
f) X / X / X X X / X / X
   mo / *wang* / *tso-ko-jen* / *hsing* / *Li*
   (Don't / forget / the man who made this song / is named / Li)
   (p. 28)

To augment the highly varied musical effects created by his selec-
tion of metrical patterns, Li Ho employed a full complement of
auditory devices, including not a few compound words to enhance
the overall auditory effect of a poem. For example:
   Alliteration *(shuang-sheng)*: *liu-lang* [li̯əu lâng in Ancient
Chinese][32] ("wander"); *hsiao-hsi* [si̯äu-ki̯ək] ("news"); *mi-meng* [miei

mung] ("misty"); *ts'en-tz'u* ⌊ts'âm ts'i] ("uneven"); *tz'u-ts'u* ⌊ts'iẹ ts'iwok] ("fretful"); *p'i-p'a* [b'ji b'a] ("lute").

Rhyming compounds *(tieh-yun)*: *lan-kan* [lânkân] ("balustrade"); *t'a-s'a* [d'âp sâp] ("suddenly rise"); *p'ai-huai* [b'uâi ruậi] ("loiter around"); *lan-shan* [lân sân] ("fading"); *fen-yün* [b'iuən iuən] ("vapor"); *lu-su* [luk suk] ("dangling").

Reduplications *(tieh-tzu)*: a combination of alliteration and rhyming compound, like *lao-lao* [lâu lâu] ("weary"); *ch'i-ch'i* [tsiei tsiei] ("chilly and lonely"); *mang-mang* [mwâng mwâng] ("far and wide"); *meng-meng* [mung mung] ("hazy"); *p'ien-p'ien* [p'iän p'iän] ("fluttering"); *hsiao-hsiao* [sieu sieu] ("whistling").

Onomatopoeia *(ni-sheng tzu)*: *lung-lung* [liung liung] ("roaring"), *ting-ting* [tieng tieng] ("ding-a-ding").

As to rhyme, Li Ho uses four hundred and forty-seven rhyme words of level tone, two hundred and forty words of oblique tone, and one hundred and twenty-five words of entering tone.[33] Words of the level tone are sonorous, reinforcing their meaning and suggesting an exalted feeling or the atmosphere of indulging in sensuous decadence, such as in his passionate poems expressing merry-making or *carpe diem* (drinking poems). Words with oblique and entering tones sound short, sharp, and screechy, usually arousing a feeling of ghostliness when they are used to describe an eerie, ominous world, as Li Ho does in his "Song of Su Hsiao-hsiao" (p. 27) and "Ballad: In the South Mountain Fields" (p. 56). Generally speaking, Li Ho tends to rhyme words with oblique and entering tones almost as frequently as those with level tones.

Among all rhyme categories, some are easier to use than others because some contain more rhyme words and hence provide the poet with more freedom of choice. Li Ho, however, does not always use those rhyme words in broader rhyme categories such as *tung*, *chen*, or *yang*; rather he tends to challenge himself with rhymes in such limited categories as *hsien, wen, ch'ing,* and *wei,* and use them as freely as other rhymes. The musical effect of Li Ho's poetry has been noted as "manipulating the melody shockingly and abruptly" *(ts'ao tiao hsien chi).*[34] This is due, in part, to his fondness for using rhyme words in oblique and entering tones and words in difficult rhyme categories.

In regard to tension between the metrical rhythm and the syntactic rhythm, the following poem provides a good example for analysis.

Bring in the Wine

Porcelain goblets,
Amber-rich dark.
From the little vat, wine drops pearls of red.
Boiled dragons, roasted phoenix, jade fat weeps,
Silk screens, embroidered curtains, surround the fragrant winds.

Blow dragon flutes!
Beat crocodile drums!
Sparkling teeth sing;
Slender waists dance.
Still more, green Spring days soon dusk;
The peach blossoms fall pell-mell like red rain:
Pray you, till day ends, drink to tipsiness;
Wine goes not to the earth on Liu Ling's grave.

[p. 132]

The following is a tonal and rhyme diagram of "Bring in the Wine."
− represents a level tone, + represents a deflected tone, / represents a pause, R represents a rhyme.

$$
\begin{aligned}
&- - / - \text{R} \\
&+ + / - \text{R} \\
&+ - / + + / - - / - \text{R} \\
&- - / - + / + - / + \\
&- - / + + / - / - - \text{R}
\end{aligned}
$$

$$
\begin{aligned}
&- / - + \\
&+ / - + \text{R} \\
&+ + / - \\
&+ - / + \text{R} \\
&+ + / - - / + / - / + \\
&- - / + + / - / - + \text{R} \\
&+ - / - + / + + / + \\
&+ / + + / - - / - + / + \text{R}
\end{aligned}
$$

This poem on the *carpe diem* theme has a pleasing rhythm, which
under close analysis is seen to be composed of the following musical
elements: (1) Uneven lines that mixed together give a variety to
rhythm. The peom consists of two three-syllable lines followed by
three seven-syllable lines and ends with an eight-syllable. (2) Vari-

ety of tone patterns and irregularity of the position of the *caesura* in each line enhance its cadence. It is interesting that words of level tone and words of deflected or oblique tone are equally balanced in number (thirty-four), but these are interwoven in such a way as to produce the highest variety in rhythm. (3) The rhymes in the first stanza are all level-toned, and seem to suggest a happy atmosphere by their sonorous sounds; those in the second stanza are oblique-toned, and seem to suggest sadness by their dull sounds, (4) In addition to alliterative compounds like *liu-li* (porcelain), *chen-chu* (pearl), *ch'ing-ch'un (green Spring)*, *luan-lo* (fall pell-mell), four words are repeated twice: *hung* (red), *lung* (dragon), *chiu* (wine), and *jih* (sun). There are also many words with the same vowel sound, such as *chung* (goblet), *nung* (rich), *lung* (dragon); *feng* (phoenix), *feng* (wind); *hsiang* (fragrance), *chiang* (soon); *chu* (pearl), *wu* (dance), *yü* (rain), etc. Thus, the euphony of this poem comes from the echo and re-echo of the polyphony of Chinese words of which the sound and the sense are consonant and mutually suggestive.

Parallelism between two lines is another feature of Li Ho's verse structure. This is simply two similar lines joined together which correspond to each other in some way. For example: "At the rocks' roots, autumn water bright,/ By the rocks' sides autumn grass thin" (p. 70); likewise, "Teeth, arranged cowries,/ Lips, saturated scarlet" (p. 113), or "Today a sweet flag flowering,/ Tomorrow a maple tree old" (p. 26).

Repetition is another noticeable structural feature. Of this there are two kinds. First, the same word is repeated in the same line in order to increase descriptive effects or to enhance the dynamic effect of action: "Cool at dawn, cool at dusk, trees like canopies" (p. 31) or "The sky thick, the earth thick, willows combing and sweeping" (p. 136). Secondly, the same word or words may be repeated in the next line, and thus the musical effect is enriched. "In your garden, don't plant trees;/ To plant trees will give you four seasons of sorrow"(p. 77),or "Repeatedly I ask the assistants: 'Is the official coming or not?'/ 'The official is not coming;the gateway is serene, deserted' " (p. 125), or "Don't wash red,/ Washed too often, the red color fades" (p. 130).

Finally, regarding structural sequence, Li Ho's poetry has been criticized for a lack of *li* (reason, logic).[35] In fact, his poetry maintains an internal consistency and follows an inner logic in its sequence. In the poem "A Ballad of Heaven," which was discussed in Chapter 2, for instance, the logic resides within the temporal development of the poem: the first four lines describe the sky *at night* (the movement of the Milky Way and the moon); the next four lines describe the heavens *at dawn* (The Princess of Ch'in rolls up the screen and Prince Ch'iao calls out dragons to plough the mist), and the last four lines describe the *rising of the sun* (roseate clouds and Hsi Ho, the charioteer of the sun-vehicle). Thus the development of the poem is actually consistent with the natural order of things. To give another example, the following poem has been criticized for its supposed "lack of unified viewpoint and logical connections".[36]

Song of Lingering Threads

Weeping willows' leaves growing old, orioles feed their young;
Lingering threads about to break, yellow bees go home.

Young man with dark sideburns, woman-with-golden-hairpins'
    guest.
In celadon pots the amber liquor sinks.

Flower terraces about to dusk, Spring takes leave;
Fallen flowers rise and perform a whirlwind dance.
Elm pods hasten each other in countless numbers;
Young Shen's green coins flank the city roads.[37]

[pp. 17–18]

The Japanese scholar Seto Yasuo comments that:

In this short poem Li Ho presents various images such as weeping willows, orioles, bees, flowers, as if trying to cram the poem with all the impressions late spring can give. However, the author's viewpoint with which he unifies all these objects does not reveal itself directly. Moreover, the author does not explain with what feeling he looks at this late spring scene. Every line of the poem is firmly separated, without any connection, either temporal, spatial, or logical. Only the images which express various feelings about late spring are arranged together as cross sections cut out from certain, so to speak, emotional moments.[38]

Initially, it must be pointed out that the theme of this poem is not at all what most commentators have interpreted it to be, a late Spring scene, but rather it expresses the helpless grieving of an aging courtesan through the outward description of late Spring.[39] As drooping willows by the roadside beckoning to passers-by are often used in classical Chinese poetry to suggest "public women," so orioles with their beautiful songs are euphemisms for singing-girls. Thus, the first line probably means that a courtesan no longer young longs to have a child of her own. "Lingering thread" *(ts'an-ssu)* in the second line may refer to fine willow twigs *(liu-ssu)*, but at the same time it may suggest her lingering passion *(ch'ing-ssu)* for an old lover who, like a yellow bee merely dallying with a flower, has returned to his own home. The next couplet may recall their relationship and their pleasures. The young man with the dark sideburns was her guest, and together they enjoyed drinking the amber liquor from celadon cups, evoking an image of luxurious idleness. The following couplet provides a transition in the poetic development. The time of pleasure does not last and now spring is passing. Gone with spring is youth; a woman past her prime is like a fallen flower. Unwilling to remain discarded, fallen flowers rise and perform a whirlwind dance with each new gust of wind; unwilling to remain deserted, she tries to detain spring—her youth—by performing her own dance: as long as flowers are dancing, even one, spring still remains and her youth is still with her. However, in the last couplet, the poet concludes that there is no way to hold back the passing of time, and spring, pleasant as it was, has gone. "Young Shen's coins" here not only refer to elm pods which look like coins but also suggest the money a courtesan's patron has spent in order to enjoy a woman's youth. As countless elm pods quickly fall, money for women and pleasure is squandered generously.

As far as the structural sequence is concerned, the poem is well organized. It seems that Li Ho has well observed the conventional structural pattern of Chinese composition: the four movements in a formal essay—opening *(ch'i)*, follow-up *(ch'eng)*, transition *(chuan)*, and conclusion *(ho)*. The poem has observed such a structural pattern so clearly that its logical connections could not be better organized.

Following Tu Mu, many readers object to Li Ho's poems for a so-called lack of *"li"* (reason, logic), and some critics, at the other extreme, try to defend him by arguing that "Li Ho's *forte* lies exactly in being beyond *li.*"[40] In fact, his poetry has its own logic which can be so unconventional that it often puzzles the reader. Today, more than one thousand years after his death, some of his lines still read like riddles, waiting for some insightful, sympathetic critic to solve.

IV *Imagery*

I follow Professor Liu's distinction between "simple imagery" and
"compound imagery": A simple image is a verbal expression that
recalls a physical sensation or evokes a mental picture without involving another object; a compound image is one that involves a
juxtaposition or a comparison of two objects, a substitution of one
object for another, or a translation of one kind of experience into
another.[41] Simple imagery is not difficult to find in Li Ho's lines.
For example in "Song of a Noble Prince in the Depths of Night"
(Kuei-kung-tzu yeh-lan ch'ü):

> Curling upward the smoke of aloes;
> Crows crying, the scene in the depths of night.
> In the meandering pond, lotus flowers wave;
> Around the waist, white jades are cold.
>
>   [p. 25]

Images like "curling upward," "smoke of aloes," "crows crying,"
"meandering pond," "lotus flowers," and "white jades" are not
merely pictures in words; they arouse emotional associations. Just as
incense curling upward or lotus flowers waving in the meandering
pond suggest a joyful atmosphere, the approaching dawn when
crows begin to cry and jade is cold indicates the aftermath of a
pleasurable night. These images also evoke various physical sensations: visual in the curling up of smoke and the waving of lotus
flowers, and auditory in the crying of crows; olfactory in the smoke
of aloes, and tactile in the coldness of white jades. All those images
are simple in the sense that they do not involve another object in
evoking mental pictures or physical sensations.

As to compound imagery, Professor Liu distinguishes four types
according to different degrees of connection between the two objects involved in the image: 1) juxtaposition, 2) comparison, 3) substitution, and 4) transference.[42]

Juxtaposition as a compound image simply puts two objects side
by side without making any overt or covert comparison between
them. In Li Ho's poetry, we find such an example: "Orchid blossoms already old, peach leaves long./ In the forbidden garden,
hanging blinds block the imperial light" (p. 60). The poet does not
compare the neglected imperial concubine to the old orchid blossoms or peach leaves, but the analogy between being old and being
neglected is subtly suggested.

Sometimes a natural phenomenon is put side by side with a human situation, to suggest an analogy or a contrast. For example "B / the parting shore, the shadow of lotus,/ A sad red left to itself drooping alone" (p. 46). In these two lines the poet does not explicitly compare a woman parted from her lover to a red lotus blossom, but the analogy between the lonely appearance of the flower and her saddened drooping image is obviously intended.

Images involving comparison of one thing with another occur often in Li Ho's poetry. The word *ju* (to be like) occurs, eighty-nine times, *ssu* (resemble) sixteen times. Comparisons are explicit when *ju* or *ssu* are used: "The rushes like crossed swords, the wind i°.ɔ perfume" (p. 30), "Clothes tattered like flying quail feathers, my horse like a dog" (p. 92), and "The peach blossoms fall pell-mell like red rain" (p. 132).

Sometimes comparisons are implicitly stated without using the words *ju* or *ssu* as in:

> The three feet of water in the chest
> Once entered a lake in Wu to behead a dragon;
> The crevice-moon, slant and bright, dew-shaving cold;
> A sash of white silk lying flat cannot be blown aloft.
>
> [p. 24]

Here a sword is first compared to "three feet of water"—it is long and it glints, then compared to a slash of moonlight through the crevice and a sash of white silk, so as to suggest the sword's cold light and heavy appearance.

Images involving substitution describe one thing as if it were another; usually the meaning is not mentioned but simply substituted by the metaphor. This kind of expression is very characteristic of Li Ho. As Ch'ien Chung-shu remarks, Li Ho has a great liking for using *tai-tz'u* (words of substitution),[43] which in Professor Liu's terminology is imagery of substitution. For example, "jade dragon" (*yü-lung*) for sword, "cold red" (*leng-hung*) for autumn flowers, "cold green" (*han-lü*) for Spring grass, "purple coins" (*tzu-ch'ien*) and "earth flowers" (*t'u-hua*) for moss. The moon is a "jade wheel" (*yü-lun*), a "sphere of light" (*t'uan-kuang*), "cold jade" (*han-yü*), a "shivering toad" (*han-ch'an*), a "shivering hare" (*han-t'u*). The sky is a "dome azure" (*yüan-ts'ang*), "empyreal green" (*k'ung-lü*), "empyreal white" (*k'ung-po*).

Images involving transference are those that attribute to objects

qualities or actions not normally associated with them. For example
in the line "An ancient bamboo with aged tips teases azure clouds"
(p. 64), the verb *je* (to provoke, incite, or tease) attributes to the
bamboo an action not normally attributable to it. But is is hard to
name the vehicle of the image: to what is the bamboo compared?
We may imagine that bamboo-tips teasing clouds are like finger-tips
teasing a cat but such comparisons will only grotesquely distort the
nature of the bamboo and spoil the aesthetic effect of the image. The
poet does not necessarily intend to compare the bamboo to anything
definite but simply to suggest the waving of the bamboo-tips in the
wind as if they were teasing the passing clouds.

Images involving transference, in many cases, have recourse to
personification. Li Ho often applies life-oriented verbs to inanimate
objects, thus giving qualities or activities of life to the insentient,
such as "die" *(ssu)*, "become old" *(lao)*, "grown gaunt" *(shou)*,
"grieve" *(ch'ou)*, "weep" *(ch'i* or *t'i)*, "sob" *(yeh)*. For example, such
lines as "Drinkers' backs cold, South Mountain dies" (p. 30), "If
Heaven had feelings, Heaven too would grow old" (p. 45), "The sun
goes down; elms' shadows grow gaunt" (p. 84), and "The choked
spring, startled, splashes out" (p. 100).

A. *Sensory and Synaesthetic Imagery*

The poet's hypersensitivity to all forms of sensory stimulation is
vividly portrayed in his notable preference for imagery of a highly
sensuous nature. Many images vividly record his visual impressions:
"The white sun goes down Mount K'un-lun,/ Radiating light as if
unravelling silk" (p. 108). The poet stands transfixed by the pulsat-
ing rhythm of light radiating from the sun in the last golden moments before it drops below the horizon, and the scene becomes a
magical one—the mountain becomes the mysterious mountains of
the west and the light rays move like threads of silk swiftly being
unravelled from a spool. Or in the line, "Wave-washed sands—how
smooth and white! / The standing horse prints a dark character" (p.
100). (The Chinese character *ma* is an ancient pictogram imitating
the form of a horse; therefore, as the horse stands on the wave-
smoothed sands, its elongated shadow appears as this character
drawn by a giant unseen hand.) Other lines are as vividly auditory or
olfactory or tactile. Images recalling birdsong, beating drums,
twanging zithers abound in his poetry. Readers of his poetry are
treated to the fragrance of flowers, banquet smells, perfumes wafted
through the air and the many textures of a rich and sensuous envi-

ronment that reach out and touch one of sensitivity, but many of these ideas have already been touched upon in the section of this chapter that deals with sensory diction.

Expanding and enriching Li Ho's already rich language is his delight in merging the senses to create images that resonate within the reader's mind on several levels. A large number of these combine several senses: visual/auditory, "Hsi Ho strikes the sun: sounds of glass" (p. 38); or "The flute sounds, blowing sun-color" (p. 80); visual/tactile, "The moon moist and lustrous, misty waves of jade" (p. 133), and, of course, "A cold emerald candle/ Consuming its light" (p. 27); visual/olfactory, "Burnt-out embers, lingering incense, the kingfisher-blue smoke curling upward" (p. 120), and "Curling upward, the smoke of aloes" (p. 25).

The auditory and tactile senses combine to create the images in "Frost heavy, drums cold, the sound cannot rise" (p. 25) and "Cold metal clangs the night watches" (p. 127). Auditory and olfactory senses merge in "A jade stove, a charcoal fire; incense tomtoms" (p. 131) and "Golden house, fragrant street, the rumble of a thousand wheels" (p. 29). The following lines contain images combining the olfactory and tactile senses: "Cold dissolves the night's drunkenness" (p. 95) and "Piercing fragrance fills the earth: the sweet flag plant" (p. 136). In some instances three or more senses are brought together, in this case visual, auditory, and tactile: "Cold redness weeping dew: the color of delicate sobbing" (p. 56) and "A female dragon chants ruefully; cold water glistens" (p. 37); likewise, "Dancing skirts, perfumed not warm" (p. 89).

B. *Kinetic Imagery*

Many of Li Ho's lines are strongly suggestive of movement, due to an abundance of kinetic images that fall into three major types: images of gyration and rotation, images describing diagonal motion, and images of inversion. Images of gyration or rotation are to be observed in the following lines: "The River of Heaven turns at night, drifting and whirling the stars" (p. 35) or "Fallen flowers rise and perform a whirlwind dance" (p. 18).

In the following lines the verb *hsieh* (inclined, sloping, leaning, slanting) is used to describe types of diagonal motion or slanting position: "Splinters of frost dance aslant up the gauze curtains" (p. 33); "Clipped wings, the small hawk slants" (p. 56); and "A torpid firefly low, the dike-path slants" (p. 56).

As Li Ho's diction shows a strong preference for hard objects, so his imagery is marked by movements of percussion, friction, rupture, and pulverization. For example: "Facing the crossroads, I beat my sword to raise a bronze-throated roar" (p. 92) or "The snapped point, scarlet and cracked, once cleaved flesh" (p. 126). Powerful, rending forces make these lines particularly forceful: "The thread of the Seven Stars snaps: Ch'ang-o dies" (p. 97) or "Just as you began to pull me up, the strong rope snapped" (p. 58).

At times, a dim and hazy world seems to have had an equal appeal for Li Ho. The word "haze" or "mist" *(yen)* occurs forty-six times in his poetry and images revealing such a poetic world are a salient feature of his writing. Characteristic of these are lines like: "A frosty bird freezes, misty-winged" (p. 102); "The sun haze rises indistinct" (p. 86); "Jade smoke, green and wet, white like pennants" (p. 124).

Many of Li Ho's poems exhibit a high degree of sensitivity to the human body and images descriptive of this abound. On the one hand, he was continually aware of his own deteriorating physical condition, and on the other, he was sensitive to the physical attributes of women: "Returned, bones thin, no color in his face,/ Disease rushing to the head, sidelocks few" (pp. 58–59); "In the brocade bed, lying down at dawn, jade skin cold;/ Dewy eyelids, not yet open, facing the dawn darkness" (p. 29); "Silken sleeves move with her hovering and dancing;/ Her fragrant sweat moistens the grains of jewels" (p. 31).

At other times, Li Ho's images reflect a comical or odd twist to his fantasies: "Aged fish leap, scraggly dragons dance" (p. 17); "Fish in rivers will not eat, standing with sand in their mouths" (p. 58); and "The water clock urges the water to choke the jade toad" (p. 36).

Many critics admire Li Ho's poetry for its surprising images. Yü-sou remarks in his *Comments on Poetry (Yü-sou shih-hua)* that "Li Ch'ang-chi's poetic line 'If Heaven had feelings, Heaven too would grow old' is so extremely singular that people believe no one can write a line to match it."[44] Hsieh Chen (1495–1575) of the Ming dynasty compares Li Ho with other T'ang dynasty poets, saying:

Li Po wrote 'Mount Ts'ang-wu collapses and the Hsiang River runs exhausted'; Chang Chi wrote 'Sweet-flag's flowers bloom, the moon remains full for long'; and Li Ho wrote 'The thread of the Seven Stars snaps;/ Ch'ang-o dies.' The key points of these three lines are the same, but Li Ho's is much more startling, extraordinary *(ch'i).*[45]

To this opinion, Hung Liang-chi (1746–1809), a Ch'ing critic, adds that: "Li Ho's line 'High on wine, [the King of Ch'in] shouts at the moon, commanding her to run backward' is indeed startling [or extraordinary]."[46]

When those critics refer to Li Ho's lines as *"ch'i"* (startling or extraordinary), they are merely commenting on his use of images that baffle one's immediate understanding or take one by surprise. This kind of imagery is similar to the "conceits" of the Metaphysical Poets of seventeenth-century England.

V *Symbolism*

A symbol differs from a compound image mainly in three ways: (1) A symbol is meant to have a general significance, whereas a compound image has only local significance. (2) A symbol is a physical object chosen to represent something abstract, whereas a compound image need not involve spiritual experience but simply two physical objects or two kinds of physical experience. (3) With a symbol, it is often difficult to identify the tenor (what is represented), though the vehicle (thing chosen to represent something else) is always named.[47]

Furthermore, there are two kinds of symbols: conventional and private or personal.[48] A conventional symbol is an object chosen by common consent or usage to represent something abstract. In Li Ho's poems, I have found quite a number of conventional symbols common to Chinese culture such as "mandarin ducks" *(yüan-yang)* for conjugal love; "drooping wings" *(ch'ui-ch'ih)* for frustrated ambition; "willow twigs" *(liu-chih)* for parting; "clouds and mud" *(yün-ni)* for wide differences; "golden fish purse" *(chin-yü-tai)* for official rank; "orchid" *(lan)* for beauty of mind.

Personal symbols are those used by a poet to represent a state of mind, a vision of the world, or the poet's own personality. Some personal symbols are in fact conventional symbols used in a personal way. In Li Ho's poems, "orchid" and "bamboo," also conventional symbols, are used as personal symbols to represent his own mind, his ambition, his prevailing character: "When I was twenty, I didn't gain the day;/ My heart sorrowful withers like a blighted orchid" (p. 92); or again, "Bamboo-sheaths fallen, the long stem peeled, jade exposed./ Look, the mother-shoot is the stuff of dragons" (p. 64).

Li Ho wrote as many as twenty-three poems on the horse, also, in many cases, a symbol for the poet's own personality. For instance, "This horse is no common horse,/ It is the very spirit of the Equine Stars" (p. 47); or the lines:

> In the great desert, sand like snow;
> Over Mount Yen-jan, the moon resembles a hook.
> When can I wear a gold headstall
> And run swiftly, treading the clear autumn?
>
> [p. 47]

Many objects in Li Ho's poetry are used as symbols representing some general or universal world, such as "firefly," "drums," and "wind." In his poetry, a firefly is a symbol of the world of death, as in "Lacquer torches welcome the newcomer,/ In the secluded field, fireflies flit pell-mell" (p. 69). Drums in Li Ho's lines symbolize time, as in "At dawn their roaring hastens the turning sun;/ At dusk their roaring calls the moon out" (p. 134). Likewise, wind serves as a symbol of an absolute conquering power over the universe as well as human life: "The south wind blows away mountains to make level lands" (p. 36), and "Thousands of years have flown with the winds" (p. 45), and "Before the winds, how many men have aged?" (p. 69).

"South Mountain" (Nan-shan) is a conventional symbol for longevity or eternity, and it is used explicitly in: "Granted your raven hair turns the color of rush flowers;/ They, along with South Mountain, will guard the Middle Kingdom" (p. 134). In the following lines the meaning is implicitly the same: "Who understands my thoughts wearied with suffering?/ Jutting forth verdure, there is only South Mountain" (p. 123). Here South Mountain represents an apathetic eternal existence that stands lofty and cold, looking unmoved upon human suffering from one generation to the next. In light of the above, the following enigmatic couplet may be taken symbolically: "At the ferry, seeing each other off, they sing 'Flowing Water';/ The drinkers' backs cold, South Mountain dies" (p. 30). Instead of interpreting ssu figuratively as "death-like silence," I take South Mountain to be a symbol and its death to be an end of the eternal, or the end of man's life. The setting of the poem is the initial symbol: a drinking party, which like human life, is temporary— either warm interactions with loved ones or encounters with strangers. Li Ho's drinkers sing a song of flowing water, a symbol of the ceaseless movement of time, and as they bid farewell to one another, their bodies feel not the warm afterglow of liquor, but a chill, and the cold presence of South Mountain.

Often on the surface, a poem may seem fairly straightforward or mundane, but on the symbolic level it can be charged with meaning. The following lines exemplify this:

> Willow catkins rush at the curtains, Spring clouds hot;
> Tortoiseshell folding screens, drunken-eyes-patterned silk.

> The eastern neighbor's butterfly flies to the western house.
> Riding a white horse, today the young man returns.

> [p. 90]

Overtly this quatrain is composed of two lines packed with images and two lines describing seemingly unrelated situations: the flight of a butterfly and the return home of a youth astride a white horse. Read symbolically it is both cohesive in its development and dramatic.

Line one is not only a seasonal allusion, but it is also packed with conventional symbols suggesting female wantonness and sexual desire, "willows" often taken to mean "public women," "Spring" itself suggesting youthful passion, and "clouds" connotative of carnal desire, especially when used together with "Spring." The effect of unrestrained passion is further amplified by the poet's choice of a verb like *p'u* (to rush) to describe the willow's action against the boudoir curtains, and an unusual stative verb like *je* (hot) to refer to the condition of the clouds. Moreover, the second line intimates a lady's boudoir with a lascivious setting: folding screens decorated with tortoise shells and tie-dyed silk with patterns as hazy as drunken eyes. Folding screens are usually used as partitions but here they seem to conceal lustful scenes. "Drunken eyes" also suggests merrymaking and ravishment, rather than simply describing the fabric of her delicate *robe-de-chambre* decorated with dazzling patterns.

The butterfly in the third line is perhaps the most heavily symbolic image in the poem. It is a transcultural, perhaps archetypal, symbol of female sexuality, of beauty, fickleness of affection, and also of the ideal, the ephemeral, and the elusive. Further, as a conventional symbol in Chinese culture, butterflies refer to the world of dreams, recalling Chuang-tzu's use of the image, also found in the West (e.g., Hawthorne's "Artist of the Beautiful"). The verb *fei* (to fly), which generally describes the motion of the butterfly, also suggests other more abstract motions such as escape, abandonment, dalliance, and fickleness, all associated with "flight."

Within the simplicity of line four is also contained a rich symbolic level of meaning. A young man riding a white horse stands for an ideal lover, the knight-errant astride a white charger. The image of the white horse is a widespread one with several meanings: the purity of the rider, the coming of a prince, a touch of dandyism. The verb *kuei* also carries the suggestion of a return *home*.

Symbolically, the poet's statement is then: while her youthful lord is away, a beautiful and passionate woman allows her affections to stray in the direction of a neighbor. However, today her young man returns, arriving on the scene unaware of the turmoil he is about to enter. The word "today" is weighted with irony, implying that prior to the moment he arrives much has already happened. The poem ends with his returning home to be surprised, leaving to the reader's imagination the task of filling in the dramatic details of his reactions to the situation and the lady's responses to him.

However, from another view, the poem may be interpreted as referring to a young man's dalliance in the gay quarters. In this instance the butterfly also suggests sexuality but from a man's viewpoint. Butterflies flit and play among flowers, suggesting one's youthful indulgences. Thus the first two lines still remain a description of sensuous luxury and carnal pleasures taking place at a courtesan's house instead of in his lady's boudoir. In short, the interpretation of the poem differs according to the different symbolic significance of the butterfly in question.

Li Ho's conscious and unconscious use of symbols is an important reason for the continued scholarly interest in his poetry more than a thousand years after his death. Even if orthodox critics wished to ignore them, they could not—due in part to his poetic skill and creative renderings, and also because of a psychological appeal that people find both difficult to identify and to disregard.

VI *Allusion*

Allusion can be divided into two types: general and specific. General allusion are those which appeal to common knowledge, beliefs, and assumptions, easily intelligible to the reader of the same cultural background. Like fossilized images and purely conventional symbols, general allusions are virtually common idioms, such as "cassia" and "toad" for the moon, "Hsi Shih" for a beauty, and "Mo Ch'ou" for a courtesan.

Specific allusions are those made to particular literary works, historical events and persons, legends, and myths. In Li Ho's extant poetry, one can find over sixty allusions to historical or legendary persons. The use of allusions can be justified only when they are

intended as an organic part of the total poetic design and serve
certain poetic purposes.

Sometimes general allusions are endowed with specific significance. In a poem expressing the relentless flight of time, Li Ho
introduces allusions to the Emperor of Ch'in and Emperor Wu of
Han by calling them by their personal names, underscoring the
mortal men behind the imperial titles: "Liu Ch'e's tomb at Mao-ling
has many inert bones;/ Ying Cheng's catalpa coffin wâstes abalone"
(p. 96). The allusions provide a sharp contrast between endless
time, the absolute conqueror of all, and its victims, ardent searchers
for immortality. Liu Ch'e, Emperor Wu of Han, was buried in the
Mao-ling tomb, and having failed to gather the Primordial Breath to
gain everlasting life, his bones proved heavy and ordinary, and lie
about in the earth. Likewise, Ying Cheng, the First Emperor of
Ch'in, died although he had made every effort to seek the Elixir of
Life. He died while on a tour of inspection, and his attendants
loaded the carriages with abalone and stock-fish to cover the smell of
the rotting corpse, fearing a rebellion might occur before they returned to the capital. Of what use was the abalone in the coffin, Li
Ho asks, now that the assiduous seeker after immortality had died?

Specific allusions are used in two major ways. First, the poet
compares himself to the person alluded to. Li Ho repeatedly compares himself to Ssu-ma Hsiang-ju, styled Ch'ang-ch'ing, who as a
poor poet and scholar eloped with the rich, young widow Cho
Wen-chün and retired to Mao-ling (in modern Shensi) after serving
as an official under Emperor Wu. The comparison is justified on
three counts. First, though he felt himself to be Ssu-ma Hsiang-ju's
equal in talent, he envied the great love there was between the poet
and Cho Wen-chün and their happy days at Mao-ling. This is seen in
the following lines:

> Ch'ang-ch'in longs for Mao-ling:
> Verdant grass drooping by the stone well;
> Playing a zither he looked at Wen-chün,
> Spring breezes blowing her sidelocks' shadows.
>
> [p. 23]

Secondly, he lamented his own as well as Ssu-ma Hsiang-ju's poverty: "To Mao-ling I returned for rest, sighing at utter poverty" (p.
64) and "Ch'ang-ch'ing reduced to poverty aggrieved at the empty
house" (p. 42). Thirdly, he felt himself the equal of the earlier poet

in poetic talent, suggesting on occasion that he was the greatest
troubadour of love in the capital since Hsiang-ju: "On Hsiang-ju's
tomb autumn cypresses have grown;/ Today in the Capital who is
the muse of love?" (p. 136).

Furthermore, Li Ho compared himself to Prince Ts'ao Chih
(192–232), younger brother of Emperor Wen of the Wei dynasty and
a representative poet of the age, because of his own imperial de-
scent: "Moth-like tresses and drunken-eyes, she prays the noble
lords,/'Pay my respects to the Imperial Scion, Ts'ao Chih'" (p. 136).
Li Ho identified himself also with Pien Jang (175–250), whose
scholarship and talent were appreciated by Ts'ai Yung (133–192), an
eniment poet and scholar of the late Han who recommended and
sponsored him for high office: "Pien Jang this morning was thinking
of Ts'ai Yung" (p. 43). Apparently Li Ho was thinking of some powerful sponsor, possibly Huang-fu Shih, who appreciated his talent
and recommended him for office as Ts'ai Yung had done for Pien
Jang.

In addition to drawing an analogy between the poet and the person alluded to, specific allusions also serve as an economical means
of presenting a situation, either drawing an analogy between the
past and the present or providing a contrast. For example, in "Song
of a Palace Doll," "A crying mole-cricket mourns the moon under
the balustrades;/ Bend-your-knees hinges and bronze door knobs
lock in Ah-chen" (p. 59). The analogous situation between the neglected palace girl and the discarded favorite of Emperor Wen of
Wei (regnet 220–226) is obvious; both were locked away in a deserted palace, consoled only by mole-crickets crying in the night,
mourning the moon.

Li Ho's use of allusions shows a specific character: historical or
legendary figures and their situations are not simply alluded to but
are represented vividly as they were originally. In other words, Li
Ho's allusions often bring the reader into the original situation in
history, legend, or myth, and thus they recreate imaginatively the
immediate tension of the moment. For example, "When the sword
was drawn, the White King of the West started,/ The Demon
Mother howled and howled in the autumn fields" (p. 25). These two
lines do not simply refer to the story of Liu Pang, founder of the Han
dynasty, who once killed a huge snake lying across his path, but
rather revive the dramatic moment when Liu Pang drew his sword.
According to legend, Liu Pang was the son of the Red King and the

snake he killed was the son of the White King of the West. After he slew the snake, not far ahead on the roadside an old woman was weeping, lamenting the death of her son. Thus Li Ho's lines express exactly the tension of the moment when Liu Pang drew out his blade, startling the White King father, while the demon mother of the snake began to howl in the autumn wilds.

Allusion is a vehicle for communication and a bond between the poet and the members of his culture in many ages. Although some are inevitably lost, many of these allusory figures and events gain added levels of meaning as they are reused in later times. In using allusion successfully, a writer is able to focus a large body of cultural experience or the details of an event into a few words or lines, creating a small drama and actually cementing the bonds of the culture itself.

VII *Conclusion*

In the above discussion I have analyzed Li Ho's poetic worlds through the kaleidoscope of his language: its imagery and euphony, its tone and rhythm, as well as its checkered and colorful patterns of composition as reflected in the reader's mind. All the specific devices of poetic language can justify themselves only to the extent that they enhance poetic effects, enrich poetic suggestions and associations, and enlarge poetic worlds. When we read a poem, we can appreciate its poetic world properly only when its language moves with a proper speed, its pictures appear in the mind in an understandable and appealing shape, and the melody flows with a proper rhythm. Therefore, the analysis of language is like a slow-motion instant replay of the moments captured in a poem; its purpose is only to help us to see the details of actions and their changes in order to appreciate the total work more effectively.

It should be evident that all the aspects of language discussed above should work together in a poem. In the following poem, the poet makes use of the full range of linguistic and literary devices available to him, thereby presenting us with an opportunity to understand better the poem and the poet.

Exhortation No. 5

At the rocks' roots, autumn water bright;
By the rocks' sides, autumn grass thin.
Assailing one's clothes the wild bamboo's fragrance;

> Thriving, drooping leaves thicken.
> Among the crags the moon returns.
> Toadlight hangs in the sky, gracefully;
> Cassia dew faces the fairy lady.
> Twinkling droplets fall from the clouds, still hanging.
> Chilled and dreary, the gardenia seeds fall.
> A mountain rift weeps clear trickles.
> Below, there is Chang Chung-wei
> Unrolling a book, his desk about to decay.

[p. 70]

The poem depicts the sterile eremetic life of a disenchanted poet living alone at the foot of a wild mountain, beside a pond hemmed in by ungroomed grasses. Autumn is the season; the grasses are dry and thin; the moon glimmers in the ripples of the lake. The parallelism of the first two lines reinforces the seasonal idea in the reader's mind and provides the poem with an underlying mood. Autumn is a time of crisp, clear air, of heightened perception so that the water appears to glisten even more clearly than ever. It is also a time when plant life goes into dormancy, creating a mood of introspection about the seasons of life, even human life, and the inevitability of death. The terrain is harsh, rocky, and inhospitable with its underbrush and crags. The next two lines describe the thick growth of bamboo through olfactory and visual images, reinforced by verb choice: the wild bamboo's fragrance is so strong it pervades or even assails the clothes.

In contrast to this earthly scene, the next four lines shift the point of view to the heavens. The moon rises as it does each night, as if a visitor returning to accompany the lonely recluse. The soft and graceful rays pour down on the mountains and the lake and the watcher below. "Toadlight" refers to a traditional Chinese legend that has it that in the moon lives a toad, a cassia tree, and a fairy lady, Ch'ang-o, who fled there after stealing the Elixir of Life. As the poet looks at the moon, it seems the fairy is standing before the cassia tree bedewed in the autumn night. The dew falls in twinkling droplets through the hanging clouds. Here the poet uses "*hsing-hsing*," a tinkling sound, to describe the falling of dewdrops. As an adjective or adverb, it means miniscule or bit-by-bit, but as a noun, it means stars, suggesting both the action and the appearance of the drops. Apparently the poet is suggesting that the stars are tiny dewdrops, falling from some heavenly place, or that dewdrops resemble stars in their sparkling movement. In short, these four lines describe the stillness and loneliness on the mountain late at night. The moon that returns is laden with symbolic meaning: it is the hidden memories of the poet's subconscious images surfacing in quiet moments that become the stuff from which poetry is made. It is the "fairy lady," the muse who has excited the minds and hearts of artists, East and West, to create—the creative impulse itself that seems to rise in fertility even in the midst of a wasteland. Perhaps the moon reminds the poet of some lost love, his own "fairy lady" who long ago stimulated him to write, whose name but not face is forgotten.

The last four lines shift the poem's view to the poet, a mortal suspended between heaven and earth, whose "pen complements creation." The poet is, or is compared to, Chang Chung-wei of the late Han dynasty, learned in astronomy and talented in poetry, who lived in a hermitage surrounded by wild underbrush. Late at night in autumn—the season of death—heralding approaching winter, the sound of dropping seeds from the gardenia is audible, and so is the weeping of the water trickling from the crevices of mountain rocks. One recalls the lines of Baudelaire:

> Il me semble, bercé par ce choc monotone,
> Qu'on cloue en grande hâte un cercueil quelque part
> Pour qui?[49]

Moved and rocked by the song of autumn, the poet awakes to the futility of his study as well as of his own life, and sees that his time has come as his desk has begun to molder.

Except for the parallelism of the first couplet, the poem's tone patterns are varied. Although it has reduplicated words like *chih-chih* (thriving) and *hsing-hsing* (stars or bit-by-bit), and some idiomatic compounds like *ch'iu-shui* (autumn water), *yeh-chu* (wild bamboo), *kuei-lai* (returns), and *chi'i-liang* (chilled and dreary), most of the compound words are not very common; *ch'an-kuang* (toadlight), *kuei-lu* (cassia dew), *yün-tou* (clouds-hanging), *shan-wen* (mountain rift), and *ch'ing-lou* (clear trickles) are relatively unusual. Furthermore, because most verbs are monosyllabic and antithesis is completely lacking, the poem yields a very strong staccato effect, as if it were a gathering of monosyllabic words. This effect is further enhanced by the form: five syllables to a line, a rhyme every two lines. This staccato effect, I think, best expresses or suggests the frustrated, unbalanced feeling contained in the poet's mind. The rhyming words are all in "deflected" tones, five falling and one rising, which certainly suggest the undulation of the poet's agony. With its staccato rhythm, the last line especially reveals the poet's deep depression, as if he were unable to contain his resentment: p'jie / siwo / ǎn- / tsiang / xiəu: !

The poem abounds in simple images suitable for direct descriptions of simple scenes of nature. Beyond the descriptions of the autumn scene, the night scene in the wilds and the man in such circumstances, there lies a deeper feeling which is suggested or evoked by these simple images. It is a feeling that the poet is declining, a feeling aroused by the autumn season. The poet sympathizes with grass that is "thin," is consoled by the moon that "returns" with eternal grace, is startled by the falling sound of gardenia seeds, and at last awakens to a recognition of the truth of life and death. It is this underlying sense that runs through the poem and provides it with a consistent structure.

Finally, the allusion to Chang Chung-wei is characteristic of Li Ho's usage. In fact, Li Ho does not so much allude to Chang Chung-wei as write the poem from Chang's viewpoint. Both Chang Chung-wei and Li Ho are one and the same, and they share the feeling expressed in the poem. Li Ho revives Chang Chung-wei who, in turn, immortalizes Li Ho by inspiring him to write such a work.

CHAPTER 4

Li Ho's Kuei-ts'ai:
An Evaluation of His Poetic Genius

HISTORICALLY speaking, classical Chinese poetry began with the *Shih Ching* (*Book of Poetry*, ca. twelfth to sixth century B.C.) and the *Ch'u Tz'u* (*Songs of the South*, ca. third century B.C.), continued with the *Yüeh-fu shih* (Music Department Songs) and the *Ku-shih* (Ancient poems) of the Han and the Wei dynasties (third century B.C. to third century A.D.), and developed into the well-known *Lü-shih* (Regulated Verse) form of the T'ang dynasty (seventh to tenth centuries). This formal development began with poems in lines of indeterminate length varying from three to seven syllables to a line, without any fixed tone patterns or rhyme schemes, and finally arrived at an extremely fixed form requiring a great amount of verbal ingenuity, the Regulated Verse.[1] It was Li Po and Tu Fu who represented the high-water mark of Chinese poetry, both in the worlds they explored and in the language with which they experimented. Tu Fu has been generally recognized as the greatest Chinese poet, whose poetic worlds are matchlessly profound and broad, and whose use of language has fully justified his fame as a great master. Apart from the quality of Tu Fu's poems, their sheer number (1,455) demonstrates his creative vigor. After Tu Fu, Chinese poetry developed a marked bifurcation. On the one hand, Yüan Chen and Po Chü-yi (772–846) emphasized poetry written in ordinary language, carrying on the plain, simple aspect of Tu Fu's poetry. On the other hand, Han Yü and his followers adopted a new point of departure, succeeding to the elaborate, abstruse aspect of Tu Fu. The former group tended to be realistic in their creation of poetic worlds, while the latter revealed a preference for extraordinary subjects and unconventional language. As a poet, of course, Li

121

Ho possesses his own characteristics, but, between these two contrasting trends, it is obvious that his poetry is closer to the latter.

From the studies of Li Ho's poetic worlds and his use of language
in the foregoing chapters, his poetic characteristics can be
generalized as follows:

1) Li Ho's poetic worlds have three dimensions: the celestial
world of immortals or divine spirits, the shadowy world of the dead,
and the human world of reality. As a matter of fact, Li Ho lived an
unhappy life of thwarted ambitions and constant frustration, and
many of his works are strongly tinged with his sufferings at the hard
hands of fate or his resentment against social injustice, although
many of his poems express purely aesthetic experience. As the
modern critic Hung Wei-fa, author of Li Ho's chronological biography, has aptly remarked, "Li Ho was much afraid of death, yet
frequently referred to death because he could not resign himself to
it." On the other hand, "He was tired of and averse to the bitterness
of this world; therefore he often fancied Heaven as well."[2] However, it seems to me that even his poems about Heaven and graves
have at heart a this-worldly attitude. In his poems about immortals,
even as his mind soars into Heaven, he often looks down upon this
world; therefore, his celestial poems are different from ordinary
roaming-with-immortals poems (Yu-hsien shih), which describe the
wandering of a poet's mind in supernatural realms where, frolicking
with immortals, it forgets all worldly affairs. The surrealistic worlds
of Li Ho's poetry often betray the poet's anguish of despair and his
dissatisfaction with this world. When despair and dissatisfaction
have reached the extreme, they tend to bring about a mental explo-
sion which threatens to involve the entire universe in the poet's
ruin. In this sense, some of Li Ho's poetry can certainly be seen to
produce a pathos of cosmic proportions.

2) With regard to the art of expression, Li Ho completely rejects
the seven-syllable regulated verse, a poetic form flourishing at that
time. Most of his poems are written in the style of yüeh-fu and
Ancient Verse: lines are irregular, rhymes are changed frequently,
and rhyme words in oblique tones are preferred. As a result, variety
in the musical flow is increased and the surprising effect of the
images is enhanced. It is this kind of free verse that serves most
properly to express the poet's profound feelings and sensitive impressions. Li Ho's poetry abounds in sensuous experiences and visual images, and at the same time possesses very strong musical

qualities. The fact that many of Li Ho's *yüeh-fu* poems were sung to the accompaniment of wind and string instruments by musicians should not be disregarded.[3] In addition, Li Ho's poetic styles have both simple and obscure aspects, just as his poetic worlds have bright and dark dimensions. The obscurity of his poetry does not so much derive from elaboration in diction or syntax as from his extraordinary associations and from the inner logic of his original ideas. If the reader has an insight into this inner logic, he will appreciate that Li Ho's poetry, in most cases, is consistent in development and well organized in terms of putting the best words in the best order.

3) From an aesthetic point of view, the intrinsic nature of Li Ho's poetry can be summed up in four words: *yu* (dark), *ming* (bright), *ch'i* (startling or extraordinary), and *li* (colorful or splendid). *Yu* and *ming* refer to Li Ho's poetic worlds, which are symbolized by his own line:

> The sputtering taper laughs in the night,
> congealing the dark and the light.
>
> [p. 33]

The poet's life resembles a lingering taper burning out its orchid oil and flickering with a dark and bright flame. Like the poet struggling with adversity, the taper sputters in the night, now and then bursting into tears and laughter, sometimes remaining still as if trying to congeal the dark and the light. In Chinese, *yu-ming* as a compound also means the human world and the nether world. Just as the taper flickering in the night simultaneously casts light and shadow, so the poet's mind projects contrasting feelings—feelings of day and night, joy and anger, life and death.

On the other hand, *ch'i* and *li* refer to Li Ho's use of language, which can be typically interpreted by such a line as: "The pen complements creation: Heaven has no merit" (p. 121). Li Ho's images often take people by surprise; his rhymes are abrupt and full of changes, his diction is colorful and strongly emotive, his language is sometimes very elaborate. All of these features are the marvelous work of his creative pen, which strives to perfect nature's creation, to startle Heaven and the gods by depriving them of credit, or even to make jealous demons cry over its exquisite workmanship.

Of course these four distinctive aesthetic qualities of Li Ho's poetry have their sources in the Chinese poetic tradition. They are traceable to *The Songs of the South*, the ancient ballads and poems of the *yüeh-fu* tradition, the court poetry during the periods of Ch'i (479–501) and Liang (502–556), and to Tu Fu. It seems to me that the "dark" aspect of Li Ho's poetry comes from *The Songs of the South*, especially "The Nine Songs" *(Chiu ko)* and "The Summons of the Soul" *(Chao-hun)*, which are full of gloomy sadness, rancor, supernatural fantasies and mysterious descriptions about divine and evil spirits. Some of his poems in this tradition are "Song of Su Hsiao-hsiao" *(Su Hsiao-hsiao ko)* (p. 27), "The Ladies of the River Hsiang" *(Hsiang Fei)* (p. 40), "High is Mount Wu" *(Wu-shan kao)* (p. 111), "Divine Strings" *(Shen hsien)* (p. 131), and "Sir, Don't Go Out the Gate!" *(Kung wu ch'u men)* (p. 118). The "bright" or less gloomy aspect of Li Ho's poetry has its source in ancient ballads and *yüeh-fu* poems which are simple in language and innocent in theme. Their expressions of human feeling are moving and artless; their satirical meaning, if any, is deep but not obscure. Li Ho's "Digging a Well in the Back Garden" *(Hou-yüan tso-ching)* (pp. 91–92) and "Children's Ballad at the City Walls of Ancient Yeh" *(Ku Yeh-ch'eng t'ung-tzu yao)* (p. 94) are typical examples.

Among the two hundred and forty-two poems that form Li Ho's complete works, more than half are modelled after *yüeh-fu* poems, and, according to the list provided by Chu Chün-yi, there are thirty-two poems which follow or adopt titles from *yüeh-fu* poems of the Han, Wei, and Six dynasties periods.[4] Li Ho sometimes borrows beautiful lines from ancient *yüeh-fu* poems either totally or with only minor changes. For example, the line "Embroidered curtains surround the fragrant winds" *(Hsiu-mu wei hsiang-feng)* in a poem entitled "Bring in the Wine" *(Chiang chin chiu)* (p. 132) is borrowed outright from an ancient *yüeh-fu* poem by an anonymous author,[5] and the line, "Don't wash red, washed too often the red color fades" *(Hsiu hsi hung, hsi to hung-se ch'ien)* (p. 130) differs from the ancient ballad of the same title only in one character: *ch'ien* instead of *tan*, probably for the sake of rhyme, but both *ch'ien* and *tan* in this context mean exactly the same thing. Sometimes Li Ho adapts a *yüeh-fu* title by altering some words to better fit the meaning he wants to express or emphasize; for example, he changes "Don't Cross the River, Sir" *(Kung wu tu ho)* to "Sir, Don't Go Out the Gate!" *(Kung wu ch'u men)* (p. 118). Sometimes he combines two old *yüeh-fu* titles to create a new one: his "Long Songs Follow Short

Songs" *(Ch'ang-ko hsü tuan-ko)* (p. 62) is apparently a combination of "Ballad: Long Songs" *(Ch'ang-ko hsing)* and "Ballad: Short Songs" *(Tuan-ko hsing)*.

The "startling or extraordinary" aspect of Li Ho's poetry is probably due in large measure to the influence of Tu Fu. As I have stated above, after Tu Fu Chinese poetry developed two tendencies: one plain and readily intelligible, aiming to make poetry popular; the other elaborate and abtruse, trying to create extraordinary lines to startle people. In point of poetic language, Tu Fu declared that he would never give up writing till he died, if he could not startle people with his words *(Yü pu ching jen ssu pu hsiu)*. [6] Echoing Tu Fu's declaration, Han Yü proclaimed that his shocking words would break demons' galls *(Hsien yü p'o kuei tan)*, [7] and Li Ho announced that his pen would complement creation and deprive Heaven of its merit.

As to the poetic worlds of the poet, Tu Fu's realism in observation of the world and his criticisms of social realities also find echoes in some of Li Ho's poems, such as "Exhortation No. 1" *(Kan-feng chih-yi)* (p. 68), "The Caves of the Huang Family" *(Huang-chia tung)* (p. 55), and "Song of an Old Jade-hunter" *(Lao-fu ts'ai yü ko)* (pp. 53–54). Furthermore, as Chou Ch'eng-chen has asserted, Tu Fu was the first poet "to apprehend the material world with the senses" and Li Ho was "best in fusing his feelings of, and responses to, life into his apprehension of the material world, in making a poem an integral experience." [8] Chou maintains that Li Ho was much influenced by Tu Fu's "sensory realism." [9]

The "colorful, splendid" aspect of Li Ho's poetry derives from the so-called "Palace Poems of the Ch'i and Liang" *(Ch'i-Liang kung-t'i shih)*, a kind of court poetry that aimed at describing the splendor and luxuries of palace life, and which flourished during the periods of Ch'i and Liang (mid-fifth century to mid-sixth century). This Ch'i-Liang court poetry characteristically employs elaborate descriptions of gorgeous decorations and furnishing in the palace, such as curtains, screens, jades, embroideries, silk, and boudoirs heavy with rich perfumes and scents. Sensitive descriptions of the delicate and amorous feelings of palace women also characterize this kind of poetry. Li Ho wrote at least forty poems in this style; some of them are about palaces, such as "Hua-ch'ing Palace" *(Hua-ch'ing kung)* (pp. 21–22) and "An-lo Palace" *(An-lo kung)* (pp. 89–90); some of them relate to historical events at court, such as "A Poem on Ch'in-

kung" *(Ch'in-kung shih)* (pp. 92–93), "Sorrow of the Ancient Terrace of Liang" *(Liang-t'ai ku ch'ou)* (pp. 117–118), "Singing-girls in
the Bronze Bird Tower" *(T'ung-ch'üeh chi)* (p. 71); and some are
concerned with the hidden sorrows of discarded palace women,
such as "Hall after Hall" *(T'ang-t'ang)* (pp. 59–60) and "Song of a
Palace Doll" *(Kung-wa ko)* (p. 59). There are two poems the poet
explicitly noted as following the style of the court poetry of Liang:
"Song of Returning from Kuei-chi" *(Huan tzu Kuei-chi ko)* (p. 18)
and "Air of an Outing among the Flowers" *(Hua-yu ch'ü)* (pp. 88–89).
This court poetry tradition was thus to contribute to Li Ho's colorful
and emotive diction and his excellent descriptions of the emotional
states of neglected women.

These four characteristic features of Li Ho's poetry seem to me to
be essentially derived from the intrinsic nature of his genius: *kuei*.
After the Sung dynasty, Li Ho was dubbed a *kuei-ts'ai*, a genius of
kuei.[10] The word *"kuei"* in Chinese has two basic meanings: 1) as a
noun referring to a ghost, a departed spirit, as in *kuei-hun* (disembodied spirits); 2) as an adjective meaning "clever," "crafty," or
"artful" as in *kuei-fu shen-kung* (extremely skillful workmanship).
Accordingly, *kuei-ts'ai* as a description of Li Ho's poetic genius has
two major implications: Li Ho was a poet who was fond of describing
"ghostly" scenes or the world of the dead, and many of his poems do
evoke "ghostly" feelings in the reader's mind; and he possessed an
almost demonic genius, which enabled him to write wonderful
poems so skillful in the use of language and so surprising in the
poetic worlds explored that he might have been a devil himself or at
least as clever as a devil.

Wada Toshio in his article about Li Ho's *kuei* poetry and its
formation is in basic agreement with these ideas, although he sum-
marizes Li Ho's usage of the word *kuei* in four ways:[11] 1) referring to
the dead or a departed spirit, as in "In an autumn graveyard, ghosts
chant Pao Chao's poems" *(Ch'iu fen kuei ch'ang Pao chia shih)* (p.
37); 2) referring to a phenomenon which occurs in connection with
the dead, as in "Ghostly rain sprinkles the empty grass" *(Kuei yü sa
k'ung ts'ao)* (p. 69); 3) referring to the gods of common belief, as in
"Sea gods and mountain spirits come to sit in seats" *(Hai shen shan
kuei lai tso chung)* (p. 131); 4) As an adjective describing exquisite,
almost inhumanly perfect workmanship, e.g., "On the thousand-
year-old stone bench, devil weavers cry" *(Ch'ien sui shih ch'uang t'i
kuei kung)* (p. 58). Wada considers the second usage (descriptive of

ghostly phenomena) to be a subordination of the first (references to the dead or departed spirits), and the fourth usage (inhuman perfection) to be irrelevant to *kuei* poetry as practised by Li Ho. Therefore, he concludes that "in the final analysis what is expressed by the word '*kuei*' in Li Ho's usage is of two kinds only: the first and the third,"[12] It seems to me, however, that such a conclusion is not justified. Rather, it is the third category (references to gods) that is an elaboration of the first (references to the dead). The divine and evil spirits of common religious belief are, in many cases, transformed from disembodied spirits of human beings or animals, gods and ghosts inhabiting a common world of fantasy and imagination.

The second category (descriptive of ghostly phenomena), on the other hand, is quite different from the first and perhaps better than the other classifications exemplifies the mysterious *kuei* quality of Li Ho's poetry. In Wada's second usage, *kuei* often serves to establish a mood of gloom or eeriness that has captivated readers for centuries. In the first usage (references to the dead), there is no common effect on the reader from the specific terms. Just as in the West various ghosts have an individual character, some being mischievous, some sorrowful, some glorious (poltergeists, the ghost of Hamlet's father, and the headless horseman), a specific *kuei* may or may not conjure up an effect of "ghostliness." So, it is the ghostly mood or sense of eeriness (Wada's second category) that a poem suggests rather than the specific subject matter it describes that impresses the mind of Li Ho's reader. Far from being a mere elaboration, the second usage of the term indicates the essential quality of his poetic world, just as the fourth usage (inhuman perfection) rather than being irrelevant is characteristic of his poetic language.

Such being the case, I believe that Li Ho has been branded a *kuei-ts'ai* for two reasons: because of the consciously ghostly and eerie atmosphere of his poems and because of their suprisingly ingenious qualities. Generally speaking, *kuei-shih* strongly appeals to the senses rather than the intellect; it is more emotive than rational. Therefore, sensuous experiences and elaborate expressions result in a passionate and resplendent style—dazzlingly beautiful words strongly appealing to the senses. For, if words are not beauteous and colorful, they cannot express the poet's feelings strongly enough to satisfy his own aesthetic instinct; if words do not strongly appeal to the senses, they probably cannot conceal the poet's inner uneasiness or cover up the bleakness of his mind. Li Ho often uses sensuous or emotive adjectives to modify colors, such as "aged red" *(lao-hung)* or "crumbling green" *(t'ui-lü)*, and thus suggests a gloomy, grievous feeling against ostensibly colorful diction, achieving a ghostly or doleful atmosphere in his poetic lines. Li Ho's *kuei-shih* are, substantially as P'an Te-yü (1785–1839) has stated, "all written with extremely colorful words, about extremely gloomy scenes; as when in a short story, a woman ghost in red makeup and dress appears among ancient palaces and desolate gardens and sends a chill through the reader's frame; if he reads under a single lamp at night, his hair will stand on end."[13]

As a *kuei-ts'ai*, Li Ho has been often mentioned together with Li Po, the poet-immortal *(shih-hsien)*, and Tu Fu, the poet-sage *(shih-sheng)*. I think these three T'ang poets represent three different poetic worlds: the nether, the celestial, and the terrestrial, respectively. Although such comparisons are necessarily general and really require further study, the attitudes toward life of all three poets can be discerned from the following three poems on the *carpe diem* theme.

Tu Fu's "The Meandering River":

Returning from Court, day after day, I pawn my Spring clothes;
Every day at the river's end, I get totally drunk and go home.
Wine debts are routine, wherever I go, there they are.
Human life past seventy since ancient times is rare.
Through the flowers the butterfly is seen deeper and deeper.
Touching the water, the dragonfly flies slower and slower.
Take my words, wind and glow of light, I float and turn with you,
For the moment, let's appreciate each other and not fall out![14]

Li Po's "Drinking Alone Beneath the Moon":

Among the flowers, a pot of wine:
Alone, drinking without company,
I lift my cup to invite the bright moon
And face my shadow to make a threesome.
Although the moon doesn't understand drinking,
And my shadow merely follows my body,
For the time being, I accompany the moon and my shadow:
Merrymaking has to be in Spring.
As I sing, the moon swings and sways;
As I dance, my shadow waves wildly.

While we're sober, let's share the companionship;
After we're drunk, each will go his own way.
Forever bound in unimpassioned friendship,
To meet again beyond the distant Cloudy River.[15]

Li Ho's "Bring in the Wine":

Porcelain goblets,
Amber-rich dark.
From the little vat, wine drops pearls of red.
Boiled dragon and roasted phoenix, jade fat weeps,
Silk screens, embroidered curtains, surround the fragrant winds.

Blow dragon flutes!
Beat crocodile drums!
Sparkling teeth sing;
Slender waists dance.
Still more, green Spring days soon draw to dusk.
The peach blossoms fall pell-mell like red rain:
Pray you, till day ends, drink to tipsiness;
Wine goes not to the earth on Liu Ling's grave.[16]

[p. 132]

Comparisons of the above three poems in terms of their poetic worlds justifies the traditional attributions of the three poets as "immortal," "sage," and "ghostly genius," and the following points may be made.

1) Tu Fu's world is realistic, touching upon the actual phases of human life in this world: attending court, incurring debts for wine, pawning Spring clothes and getting drunk daily. He looks outward upon the world, appreciating its natural beauty, and he wishes to live harmoniously and peacefully with it even if only momentarily. He realizes that impermanency is the nature of all things, and life, short as it is, is full of beautiful things for man to appreciate. Thus Tu Fu shows his wisdom of life as a sage or a philosopher.

2) Li Po's world is fantastical, narcissistic, unworldly. He seems to be completely carefree, drinking a pot of wine among the flowers, dancing with the moon, and talking to his own shadow. That is the way he enjoys life while it is Spring. He looks toward the sky, wishing to maintain an everlasting friendship with the moon and to meet it again among the clouds. The poet's mind is carried away by his own fantasies and becomes disconnected from reality like an

immortal or fairy who is said to live on air. Thus this poem shows a typical aspect of Li Po's mind as that of an other-worldly poet.

3) Li Ho's world is pleasure-seeking, hedonistic, but ends on a somewhat gloomy note. It strongly appeals to sensuousness; all the senses, visual, auditory, olfactory, tactile, and gustatory, play in concert in this poem. It seems that only through his senses is the poet able to grasp the world, that only through sensuous stimulations is he able to enjoy life to his heart's content, to forget human sufferings even if only temporarily, and to escape from the relentless plunder of time. His eyes look downward to the grave. Even at the height of enjoyment, he never fails to remind himself of the end of all pleasures, because he knows well that time is constantly extorting life from humankind and the world; both are destined to come to an end. This poem shows that the poet, however hard he tries to enjoy life, is always oppressed by the passage of time and haunted by the shadow of death.

In terms of the breadth and variety of poetic worlds explored, Li Ho's poetry cannot compare with Li Po's or Tu Fu's, for he has left behind only two hundred and forty-two poems, while to Li Po and Tu Fu 1,004 and 1,455 poems are attributed respectively.[17] As Suzuki Torao maintains, Li Ho is only an illustrious poet *(ming-chia)* rather than a great master *(ta-chia)*.[18] A *ta-chia* demonstrates versatility in varied accomplishments: many-sided subject matter, wide-ranging poetic worlds, and diverse forms; an adept not only in quantity but also in the quality of poetry, not only in the worlds originally explored but also in the use of language successfully explored. A *ming-chia* excels other poets in his speciality. Li Ho is best known for his *kuei* poetry which is full of ghostly atmosphere and startling images. Although he can hardly be recognized as a great master, Li Ho's position in the history of Chinese literature is unique and beyond question.

In the past several decades Li Ho has been compared to or mentioned together with many Western poets and considered, as the modern poet-critic Yü Kuang-chung puts it, an "unintended precursor" of many Western literary "isms."[19] Professor David Ch'en has also likened his life to John Keats's (1795–1821) in its "poverty, illness, frustration," causing these two poets to be "congenial in spirit and similar in style," because "the essential and common experience of life of the two poets is suffering, and suffering in a devoted and persistent poetic career has refined their works into a poetry of intensity."[20] According to A. C. Graham, Li Ho reminds many Western readers of Baudelaire or a nineteenth-century Satanist, because of "his apparently familiar constellation of pessimism, voluptuousness, aestheticism, and an imagination haunted by dark force."[21] It has also been pointed out that Li Ho's imagery is Surrealistic, because it is congruent with the "classifications of Surrealist images" developed by André Breton (1896–1966), especially the image which "possesses the character of a hallucination" and "implies the negation of some elementary physical property."[22] Thus he is further seen to be a Surrealist because he was "able to organize heterogeneous images into a homogeneous mood with a way of imagination which Shakespeare calls 'fine frenzy'."[23] By the same token, he is taken to be an Imagist because "of the six credos of Imagism, Li Ho anticipated all except the one that insists on the use of daily speech."[24] Moreover, many Chinese scholars consider him an aesthete because his poetry aims only at "beauty" and is richly stored with "sheer silk and perfume," "romantic moods and sensuous feelings" as well as "beauteous words and sonorous rhymes";[25] in short, because he "tried to build a palace of art in this human world."[26] In addition, Li Ho is seen to "have a prophetic place in the niche of Symbolism. For we find in Li Ho two remarkable traits of the school: suggestiveness and fusion of sense experiences."[27]

Thus, Li Ho proves to be a most interesting subject for the comparative study of Chinese and Western literatures. The fact that Li Ho's poetry can give rise to such different interpretations reflects the multifaceted nature of his poetry. Although there is some truth in each comparison mentioned above, these are no more than impressionistic comments, none being based on a comprehensive and thorough study of the poets compared or the theories adduced. Strictly speaking, an extensive and detailed study of Li Ho in comparison with various Western poets or in terms of modern Western literary theory still remains to be done.

Notes and References

The transcriptions of Chinese words are given in the Wade-Giles System, with minor modifications (e.g. *yi* for *i*). Diacritical markings, with the exception of the umlaut, have been omitted for typographical reasons. For the purpose of the discussion of euphony in Chapter 3, I have employed Bernhard Karlgren's system of transcription for archaic Chinese. All translations, unless otherwise specified, are my own.

Chapter One

1. See *New T'ang History*, *chüan* 203, K'ai-ming edition, pp. 4104–4105, and *Old T'ang History*, *chüan* 137, K'ai-ming edition, p. 3452.

2. There were three Princes of Cheng of the T'ang royal house. Scholarly opinion differs as to which Prince of Cheng Li Ho's family was descended from. See M. T. South, *Li Ho, A Scholar-official of the Yüan-ho Period (806–821)* (Adelaide: Libraries Board of South Australia, 1967), pp. 96–100.

3. *Li Ho ko-shih-pien* [Songs and Poems of Li Ho] (Taipei: National Central Library, 1971), p. 147. Hereafter, references to the original poems in this edition are indicated by page numbers in brackets following the translation.

4. See Wang Ting-pao (*ca.* tenth century), *T'ang chih-yen* [Collected Anecdotes of T'ang], in *Ts'ung-shu chi-ch'eng (ch'u-pien)* [Collection of Collections of Works], *chüan* 10, pp. 96–97.

5. See Chang Ku (a T'ang writer), *Yu-hsien ku-ts'ui* [Leisure Advocates] in *T'ang-jen shuo-hui* [Collected Stories of the T'ang People] (Shanghai: Sao-yeh shan-fang, 1930), Vol. II, p. 2a.

6. *Yüeh-fu* refers both to songs collected by the Music Bureau *(Yüeh-fu)* in the Han dynasty and later songs and poems modelled after them.

7. About the circumstances and details of taking an imperial examination, see South, *Li Ho*, pp. 245–48.

8. Hsiang-yang is a place in Hupei province especially famous for its knights-errant. As Suzuki points out, one edition (he does not specify which) reads Ch'ang-an for Hsiang-yang. Li Ho might have changed it later

31. M. T. South suggests that because in several poems Li Ho had been extremely critical of the eunuch-commander Tʻu-tʻu Chʻeng-tsʻui, and because this fact would surely have become widely known, when Tʻu-tʻu returned to the capital, Ho may not have commanded sufficient backing to be reappointed after his first term of office expired. [M. T. South, *Li Ho*, pp. 303–304.]

32. The sword of Liu Pang (247–195 B.C.), the first Emperor of Han, was an extraordinary blade that, according to legend, had magical powers and flew away, breaking through the roof, when a fire occurred. Li Ho is here comparing it to himself as no ordinary man.

33. "A Short Biography of Li Chʻang-chi" included in *Li Chʻang-chi ko-shih* [Songs and Poems of Li Chʻang-chi] annotated by Wang Chʻi. See *San-chia pʻing-chu Li Chʻang-chi ko'shih* [Songs and Poems of Li Chʻang-chi Commented and Annotated by Three Scholars] (Shanghai: Chung-hua shu-chü, 1959), pp. 13–14.

34. M. T. South states that Li Ho and his fellow literati of the mid-Tʻang period expressed their opinions about the state of society in *yüeh-fu* style poems and that "the last two lines . . . certainly suggest that the poet himself considered that his exclusion from office may have been the result of his outspokenness." [*Li Ho*, p. 304].

35. Chʻeng-chi: the ancestral home of the imperial family of Tʻang. Li Ho never forgot his noble origins.

36. Chih-yi Tzu-pʻi: a name taken by Fan Li (fifth century B.C.), a great statesman of Yüeh, when he retired from politics to become a hermit.

37. King of Chʻin: the first Emperor of Chʻin (246–214 B.C.) here standing for the ruling Emperor Hsien-tsung *(regnet* 805–820). See Chapter 2, part 1, note 7.

38. Lung-hsi: same as Chʻeng-chi, ancestral home of the imperial family of Tʻang.

39. Chao-chʻeng: a former name for Lu-chou, which was part of the former territory of Chao.

40. The last scene of Li Ho's death, described in the "Short Biography of Li Ho," was not simply invented by the author Li Shang-yin. He emphasizes that he was told the story by Ho's elder sister and that she was not the sort of person who could have fabricated it; what she reported about the incident was certainly what she had observed.

41. The cause of Li Ho's fatal disease is unknown. However, Yao Wen-hsieh, a commentator of the seventeenth century, asserts that "Li Ho's disease was certainly due to women, because he died young" [*San-chia pʻing-chu Li Chʻang-chi ko-shih*, p. 211]. Pursuing Yao's line of thought on this, J. D. Frodsham suggests that Li Ho died of tuberculosis. He says, "This [Yao's] theory may, of course, be simply a piece of Confucian moralizing. But since pulmonary tuberculosis notoriously exacerbates sexuality, my own guess would be that Yao was right" [*The Poems of Li Ho*, p. xxvii]. According to Dr. Kao-liang Chou, Professor of Medicine at Stanford

University, this popular belief in heightened sexuality among persons suffering from tuberculosis is without scientific basis.

Chapter Two

1. Kamio Ryūsuke. *"Yoru no shijin—Ri Ga no hikari no kankaku ni tsuite"* [The Poet of Night: on Li Ho's Sensibilities with Regard to Light], *Chūgoku Bungei Zadankai Nōto* [Notes of Symposia on Chinese Literature], No. 10 (1957), p. 16.

2. Seto Yasuo. *"Ri Ga zatsuron—Ri Ga no ishiki sekai"* [On Li Ho: His World of Perception], *Shūkan Tōyōgaku* [Chinese and Oriental Studies], No. 16 (1966), p. 79.

3. As Kōzen Hiroshi acknowledges, "It seems we Japanese are apt to be pleased by such a manner of expression." See his review of books by Arai Ken and Yeh Ts'ung-ch'i in *Chūgoku Bungaku-hō* [Journal of Chinese Literature], No. 12 (1960), p. 177.

4. Orchids and some other fragrant herbs have traditionally been interpreted as symbolic of a virtuous or gifted individual as well as of a man's moral excellence or influence. See David Hawkes' "Additional Notes on 'The Fragrant One,'" in *Ch'u Tz'u: The Songs of the South* (Oxford: The Clarendon Press, 1959), pp. 212–213.

5. Therefore, Eliot asserts, "When the external facts, which must terminate in sensory experience, are given, the emotion is immediately evoked," in "Hamlet and His Problems," *Selected Essays* (New York: Harcourt, Brace and Company, 1932), p. 125.

6. "Long song" and "short song" are originally titles of *yüeh-fu* ballads, most of them having the brevity of life as a theme. Some commentators argue that "long" or "short" refers to the span of life, while others contend that it refers to the length of the songs. Here Li Ho borrows the titles and combines them: "long song" apparently stands for *"kao-ko"* (singing aloud passionate songs) and "short song" for *""k'u-yin"* (chanting painful songs) as Yeh Ts'ung-ch'i suggests in his *Li Ho shih-chi* [Poems of Li Ho] (Peking: Jen-min wen-hsüeh ch'u-pan-she, 1959), p. 131.

7. According to Yao Wen-hsieh's commentary, the King of Ch'in stands for Emperor Hsien-tsung, because both exercised power and pursued immortality. Wang Ch'i notes that at that time the reigning Emperor Hsien-tsung was in the land of Ch'in; therefore he was compared to the King of Ch'in. Morise Toshizō disagrees with Yao and Wang and suggests that the allusion refers to Emperor T'ai-tsung of T'ang. See *"Ri Ga 'Shin'o inshū' o megutte"* ["About Li Ho's 'The King of Ch'in Drinks Wine'"] included in *Chūgoku bungaku gogaku ronshū* [Studies in Chinese Literature and Linguistics] (Tokyo: Chikuma shobō, 1974), pp. 433–46.

8. T'ien Wu: god of the sea. According to the *Shan-hai-ching* [Classic of Mountains and Seas], *chüan* 9, he was a monster of eight heads with eight faces, eight legs and eight tails, and a green-yellow back.

9. The Queen Mother of the West: a goddess supposedly dwelling on Mount K'un-lun; her immortal peaches bloom and bear fruit only once every three thousand years.

10. Ancestor P'eng: a legendary official of the Yin dynasty (1766–1122 B.C.), who was said to have lived more than eight hundred years, from the Hsia dynasty to the end of Yin. Shaman Hsien: a shaman during the time of the legendary emperor Yao (or a sorcerer who is said to have lived at the time of the Yellow Emperor or during the Yin dynasty), who could forecast the date of one's death.

11. Ting Tu-hu (Governor Ting): title of a mournful *yüeh-fu* ballad. When the son-in-law of the Emperor Wu of the Liu-Sung dynasty (*regnet* 420–422) was killed, the emperor ordered Governor Ting Wu to take charge of funeral arrangements. The unhappy wife of the dead prince was so concerned with her late husband's funeral that she called in Governor Ting from time to time to inquire into the details. Whenever she asked him a question, she sighed and exclaimed, "Oh, Governor Ting!" Her voice was so sad that people in later times made a *yüeh-fu* on this event. See "*Yüeh-chih*" [Treatise on Music], No. 9, in *Sung Shu* [History of the Former Sung], *chüan* 19, Kai-ming edition, p. 1474. Li Ho's meaning in this line is ambiguous. It may address a Governor Ting who drinks with the poet, or it may refer to the *yüeh-fu* song which stands for a sad song in general. Judging from the context, here "Ting Tu-hu" seems to stand for a song of fidelity to one's lord or master.

12. The Lord of P'ing-yüan (third century B.C.): the Prince of Chao during the period of the Warring States (403–221 B.C.), who was famous for his munificence in supporting thousands of retainers and for his ability to humble himself before men of ability.

13. Although the Lord of P'ing-yüan's grave is not in the state of Chao, this interpretation is justifiable because he was a prince and prime minister in the state of Chao.

14. In ancient times a jade water clock was made in the form of a dragon with water dripping from its mouth into the mouth of a jade toad.

15. Lady Wei: a beautiful woman in general or the zither player referred to in the seventh line in particular. Women in the state of Wei, such as Nan Tzu of the Chou dynasty and Wei Tzu-fu of the Han, were considered to be particularly beautiful.

16. In "*Ch'ang-ku shih*" (A Poem of Ch'ang-ku), p. 102, Li Ho also refers to himself as a "fretful man from Ch'eng-chi (*tz'u ts'u Ch'eng-chi jen*). It seems that Li Ho was very conscious of his own restless state of mind.

17. Spinner *(lo-ṵei):* a cricket-like insect whose incessant cry sounds like the whirl of a spinning wheel; also called "*suo-chi*" or "fang-chih-niang."

18. Before the invention of paper (second century A.D.), Chinese characters were written on strips of bamboo from which the green outer layer had been stripped.

19. Pao Chao (405?–466): a poet of the Liu-Sung period (420–479), who wrote a poem on graveyards *("Tai hao-li hsing")* and an elegy entitled *"Tai wan-ko,"* both lamenting human mortality. Pao Chao and Li Ho shared similarly frustrated official lives and poetic characteristics. Li Ho seems to have identified with Pao Chao as a poet with a similar fate, since both express in their poetry vehement resentment and a pathetic feeling capable of moving ghosts to chanting and tears.

20. It is said that the Emperor Ch'in Shih-huang-ti built a stone bridge stretching thirty *li* into the sea in order to watch the sun rise.

21. Pillars of bronze: either the pillars on which stood the bronze Immortal holding a dew-plate, or those legendary bronze pillars on Mount K'un-lun, known as the "sky pillars" *(t'ien-chu)*, standing so high as to touch the sky.

22. Flying Swallow (Chao Fei-yen, ?–2 B.C.): the beautiful consort of Emperor Ch'eng of the Former Han *(regnet* 32–7 B.C.); here she symbolizes imperial concubines in general.

23. Emperor Wu of the Former Han *(regnet* 141–87 B.C.) and the first Emperor of Ch'in *(regnet* 247–210 B.C.) were both notorious for their enthusiastic pursuit of immortality.

24. South Mountain: a mountain to the south of Ch'ang-an, used as a symbol of longevity, as in the felicitous wish for one's birthday: *"Shou pi Nan-shan"* (May your age be as old as South Mountain).

25. Mount K'un-lun: a mythical mountain in western China.

26. Daylight Valley: a mythical valley in the east which becomes bright when the sun rises, hence used as the name of the place where the sun is supposed to rise.

27. The Sunglow Tree: according to the *Shan-hai-ching, chüan* 17, in the great wilds there were the Heng-shih Mountains, the Chiu-yin Mountains, and the Hui-yeh Mountains, on which stood a red tree with green leaves and red blossoms which was called the *Jo*-tree *(Jo-mu),* of which *jo* probably means "dubious" or "look-alike." Many commentators believe that the *Jo*-tree is in the extreme west of Mount K'un-lun and that Li Ho made an error when he wrote, "In the eastern sky there is a *Jo*-tree" *(T'ien-tung yu Jo-mu)* in the poem *"K'u chou tuan"* (Suffering from the Shortness of Days) [p. 96]. However, the modern scholar Li Chia-yen contends that *Jo-mu* and *Fu-sang* are one and the same, both referring to the rosy clouds in the sky when the sun rises or sets. So, *Jo*-tree or Sunglow Tree can also occur in the eastern sky. See *"Fu-sang wei yün-hsia shuo"* (A Study of the *Fu-sang* as Rosy Clouds) in *Ku'shih ch'u-t'an* [A Preliminary Study of Ancient Poems]. (Shanghai: Ku-tien wen-hsüeh ch'u-pan-she, 1957), pp. 67–70.

28. According to legend, ten suns came out together during the reign of Yao, and all the trees and grasses withered. Emperor Yao ordered the great archer Yi to shoot down the offending suns but he hit only nine. The nine crows in these suns died, losing their feathers and wings.

29. See Morohashi's *Dai Kan-Wa Ji-ten*, 31458: Nos. 13–18.

30. *Confucian Analects*, Book IX, "Tzu Han." See James Legge, *The Chinese Classics* (Hong Kong: Hong Kong University Press, 1960), Vol. I, p. 222.

31. "L'Ennemi" in *Les Fleurs du Mal:* "Alas! Alas! Time eats away our lives./ And the hidden Enemy who gnaws at our hearts,/ Grows by drawing strength from the blood we lose." Translated by William Aggeler. *The Flowers of Evil* (Fresno: Academy Library Guild, 1954), p. 41.

32. In traditional Chinese thought, the *hun* comes from heaven and the *p'o* comes from the earth; the union of the two animates the human body. Cf. "The intelligent spirit returns to heaven; the body and animal soul return to the earth" *(Hun ch'i kuei yü t'ien, hsing p'o kuei yü ti)* from the *Li Chi* [Book of Rites], translated by James Legge (New York: University Books Inc., 1967), p. 444. Kobayashi Taichirō interprets an artist's mind in terms of *hun* and *p'o* and maintains that Li Ho is more of a poet of *p'o* because his mind tends to go down to the earth. See Harada Kenyū, *Ri Ga Kenkyū* [Li Ho Studies], No. 8 (1973), p. 94, and Kobayashi Taichirō, *Geijutsu no rikai no tamei ni* [Toward an Understanding of the Arts] (Kyoto: Tankōsha, 1973), pp. 152-153.

33. The Chinese believed that a hare, a toad, a cassia tree, and a palace were on the moon.

34. According to legend, Ch'ang-o stole the elixir of immortality from her husband Yi, the Archer, and fled to the moon. This line refers either specifically to Ch'ang-o or to goddesses in general whom Li Ho might meet on the moon.

35. The Three Mountains: the three legendary islands in the Eastern Sea where immortals were thought to live.

36. In ancient times, China was divided into nine states or provinces known as *chiu-chou*.

37. I am indebted to Professor William Lyell, Stanford University, for this stimulating interpretation.

38. "When the P'eng Bird journeys to the southern darkness, the waters are disturbed for three thousand *li*. He beats the whirlwind and rises ninety thousand *li*, setting off on the sixth month gale. Wavering heat, bits of dust, living things blowing each other about—the sky looks very blue. Is that its real color, or is it because it is so far away and has no end? When the bird looks down, all he sees is blue." From "Free and Easy Wandering" in *The Complete Works of Chuang-tzu*, translated by Burton Watson (New York and London: Columbia University Press, 1968), p. 29.

39. The Princess of Ch'in: Nung-yü, daughter of Duke Mu of Ch'in. She was married to Hsiao Shih, an expert at playing the *hsiao* (flute), who taught her to play in imitation of a phoenix's cry. After several years, the music she made was so beautiful that phoenixes came to perch on the palace roofs. One day the couple flew away with the birds. In Li Ho's imagination,

Nung-yü flew to heaven, where she planted a paulowmia tree in front of their window, because phoenixes were said to favor only paulowmia trees as a resting place.

40. Prince Ch'iao: a son of King Ling of Chou (*regnet* 571–543 B.C.), who liked to play the *sheng* pipes, also in imitation of the cries of phoenixes, and who finally became an immortal.

41. Green Isle: a legendary island in the Southern Sea, full of luxuriant trees and mythical plants which could be used to make the Elixir of Life; it was said to be a favorite haunt of immortals.

42. Hsi Ho: the charioteer of the sun, who rides in a chariot drawn by six dragons or horses.

43. Su Hsiao-hsiao: a famous singing girl from Ch'ien-t'ang (Hangchow) during the Southern Ch'i dynasty (479–501).

44. See *Yü-t'ai hsin-yung*, *chüan* 10, S*su-pu pei-yao* edition, p. 74.

45. I owe the following interpretation to Dr. James Miller of Berkeley, California.

46. Ho-p'u: a pearl center and trading place during the Later Han period (25–220), in today's Kwangtung province.

47. Lung-chou: same as Lung-yang in Hunan. Li Heng of the period of Wu (222–280) planted a thousand orange trees at Lung-yang without the knowledge of his wife. On his deathbed, he told his children: "Because your mother didn't want me to manage the household, we have been so poor. But now in my native place I have a thousand 'wood slaves' to produce wealth for you. I hope you won't be pressed for a living." See *San-kuo chih* [History of the Three Kingdoms], *Wu-shu* [History of Wu], *chüan* 3, K'ai-ming edition, p. 1038a. Here Li Ho seems to use "wood slaves" only as a substitution for "oranges" without further implication.

48. *Tu Kung-pu chi* [Collected Works of Tu Fu], in *Ssu-pu pei-yao*, *chüan* 2, pp. 14a-b.

49. "The first voice is the voice of the poet talking to himself—or to nobody. The second is the voice of the poet addressing an audience, whether large or small. The third is the voice of the poet when he attempts to create a dramatic character speaking in verse; when he is saying, not what he would say in his own person but only what he can say within the limits of the imaginary character." See T. S. Eliot, "Three Voices of Poetry," *On Poetry and Poets* (New York: Farrar, Straus and Cudahy, 1957), p. 96.

50. Indigo Stream: in Mount Indigo Field (*Lan-t'ien shan*) in Shensi, which is also called Jade Mountain (*Yü-shan*), it is specially known for emerald-colored jade.

51. According to legend, Emperor Wang of Shu whose personal name was Tu Yü, had a love affair with his prime minister's wife and died of shame. After his death, his soul was metamorphosed into the cuckoo, which is said to cry and shed blood in late spring. Its sound is so sad and moving that it makes a traveler homesick.

52. *Wei Su-chou chi* [Collected Works of Wei Ying-wu] in *Ssu-pu pei-yao, chüan* 10, pp. 4b–5a.

53. "Bamboo horse" usually refers to a bamboo hobbyhorse for children. Yeh Ts'ung-ch'i suggests it indicates the aboriginal tribe's bravery by showing such a playful attitude toward fighting. Wang Ch'i comments that it might be the name of a particular type of horse or some type of transport vehicle used by the natives.

54. Jung-chou: modern Jung county in Kwangsi province. The character "*ch'a*" in the last line is a *patois* for "people" used by the natives of Jung-chou.

55. About Emperor Hsien-tsung's indulgence in Taoist drugs and the so-called "Elixirs of Immortality," see M. T. South, *Li Ho*, pp. 375–377.

56. The original text reads "the ninth year," which is a mistake probably due to the similarity of the characters "*wu*" (five) and "*chiu*" (nine).

57. This line has been admired by countless later poets. The comment in Ssu-ma Wen-kung's *Shih-hua* [Comments on Poetry] quoted by Wang Ch'i goes as follows: "Li Ho's line 'If Heaven had feelings, Heaven would also grow old,' is striking and remarkable and defies all attempts to match it. Shih Man-ch'ing wrote 'If the moon had no regrets, the moon would be always full,' to form an antithetical couplet. People considered it a redoubtable equal." However, Wang Ch'i concludes that by considering these two lines carefully, one will realize that after all there is a distinction between spontaneity and deliberation and they should not be admired on the same level. See Wang Ch'i, *Li Ch'ang-chi ko-shih*, p. 67.

58. See Chapter I, Note 41.

59. Wang Ch'i, *Li Ch'ang-chi ko-shih*, p. 84.

60. *Ibid.*, p. 85.

61. Wang Ch'i interprets the carp-wind as the wind which blows between spring and summer in order to correspond with the plum-rains, but, as Suzuki Torao points out, Wang Ch'i takes no account of the lotus flowers which cannot be growing old at that time. Therefore, Suzuki takes the carp-wind to mean the wind in the ninth month and interprets the plum-rains as the time when the woman parted from her husband. However, Suzuki's interpretation has its own problem: he glosses over the verb *chi* (to send) and takes it to mean "to give." One can *send* something to someone *from* whom one is *parted*, but not to someone *with* whom one is *parting*. Yeh Ts'ung-chi follows Wang Ch'i's interpretation but he takes lotus to mean leaves instead of flowers; in that case, he misses the meaning I have suggested.

62. Since caltrop-blossoms (*ling-hua*) are purple not white, here *ling-hua* stands for a mirror originally in the shape of the flower known as *ling-hua-ching*.

63. Some commentators take *tuan-ying* as "broken cap-tassel" referring to the story of a guest of King Chuang of Ch'u (*regnet* 613–591 B.C.).

During a party all the candles suddenly blew out. A guest took the chance to flirt with one of the King's ladies, who became angry, tore off the guest's cap-tassel, and told the King what had happened. In order not to disgrace the quest, the King ordered all the guests to tear off their cap-tassels, and then had the candles lighted again. See Liu Hsiang, *Shuo Yüan* (Taipei: Shih-chieh shu-chü, 1958), *chüan* 6, p. 47. Some commentators think that this story has nothing to do with the poem in question. However, it may refer to the free-and-easy merrymaking of a courtesan and her guest, who left his broken cap-tassel with her as a keepsake.

64. Hsi Shih: a famed beauty of the Spring and Autumn era (722–484 B.C.), who was offered to Fu Ch'ai, King of Wu, by Kou Chien, the deposed King of Yüeh, as a distraction to help Kou Chien conquer Wu and restore his state.

65. The second line is rather obscure. Although Ch'iu Hsiang-sui, a commentator of the seventeenth century, pointed out that *pan ch'en t'an* means "not completely relying on *ch'en* (aloeswood) and *t'an* (sandalwood)," and Tseng Yi, an earlier commentator, suggested that "it describes the fragrance (of her hair)," many later commentators have interpreted this line quite differently: (1) Suzuki Torao comments that *t'an*, not understandable in this context, probably is a mistake for *t'an* (a carpet), and thus he interprets the line like this: "Her fragrant topknot and falling chignon have half sunk in the carpet," mistaking the noun *ch'en* (aloeswood) as the verb "to sink." (2) Yeh Ts'ung-ch'i takes *ch'en* for *chen* (a pillow), and thus he interprets the line to mean: "Her topknot and chignon fall awry and cover half of the sandalwood pillow." (3) Arai Ken quotes a line from one of Li Yü's (937–978) lyrics, "*Yi-hu-chu*," and interprets *t'an* as "pink" and *ch'en* as "thickness of color," taking the phrase to mean "deep pink lipstick or rouge has half faded." (4) Saitō Shō disagrees with these interpretations and simply takes *ch'en-t'an* to mean perfume in general, thus interpreting the line as "the perfume of aloeswood and sandalwood floats half in (or in the middle of) her falling topknot." (5) J. D. Frodsham translates the line as "Scented coils of her falling chignon/ Half aloes, half sandalwood." In fact, Ch'iu Hsiang-sui's original interpretation makes the best sense: her fragrant hair is half scented by aloes and sandalwood. In other words, her hair's fragrance is partly due to the perfume she applies, partly due to nature.

66. See Fang Fu-nan's comment, *San-chia p'ing-chu Li Ch'ang-chi ko-shih* (Li Ho's Poems Annotated and Commented by Three Scholars) (Peking: Chung-hua Shu-chü, 1959), p. 324.

67. *Ibid.*

68. Yao Wen-hsieh, *San-chia p'ing-chu Li Ch'ang-chi ko-shih*, p. 276.

69. This breeze is an allusion to King Hsiang of Ch'u. When the king roamed about the Orchid Terrace Palace, there was a rustling of the wind, and he opened his front lapel, faced the wind, and said, "How pleasant the wind is!" [See Sung Yü, *"Feng-fu"* (A *Fu* on the Wind), *Wen-hsüan, Ssu-pu*

pei-yao edition, *chüan* 13, p. 1b.] Hence, the breeze of the Orchid Terrace indicates an agreeable breeze.

70. Wang Ch'i, *Li Ch'ang-chi ko-shih*, p. 82.

71. "In ancient times when Ch'ang Chieh created the written script, Heaven rained down grain and ghosts cried at night." See *Huai-nan-tzu*, *chüan* 8, *Ssu-pu pei-yao* edition, p. 4b.

72. Suzuki, *Ri Chōkichi kashishū*, p. 208.

73. Based on a different edition of the text which gives the title of the poem as "*Lo-fu chiao yü ko p'ien*" instead of "*Lo-fu shan-jen yü ko p'ien*," Michael Fish interprets the cloth as a gift from a lady (Lo-fu is the name of a beautiful woman who appears in an ancient *yüeh-fu* poem) rather than from the old immortal of the Lo-fu Mountains. He also takes the wind in the second line to mean "lust" or "desire," and "Wu blade" and "Wu beauty" in the last line to suggest the poet and his lady, recalling the sexual connotations of a man's "virile knife" and a woman's "sheath" which appear in the *Yu hsien k'u* [Roaming in the Cave of the Immortals] by Chang Wen-cheng. He concludes that "What is to be maintained here is the strength of the possibility that the poet did in fact mean the poem to also be read in this way." [*Mythological Themes in the Poetry of Li Ho*, p. 99]. I think this interpretation is too farfetched to be persuasive. First of all, the edition [*Li Ch'ang-chi wen-chi*] on which this interpretation depends contains more misprints than any other. It is clear that in this particular poem, Lo-fu (the lady's name) is simply a mistake for the name of the mountain, because the fourth line of the poem reads explicitly *Po-lo lao-hsien* which refers to the immortal from the Lo-fu Mountains in Po-lo county, and has nothing to do with Lo-fu the lady. As the title of the poem is misunderstood, this interpretation of the poem itself is distorted.

74. Wu Kang: All scholars agree that Wu Chih in the original line is simply a mistake for Wu Kang, the Taoist immortal, who was exiled to the moon. He is punished for an error made in the process of attaining immortality with the endless labor of pruning the lunar cassia tree which is restored to its original shape as soon as it is cut.

75. Ch'ien Chung-shu, *T'an yi lu* [Comments on Art] (Shanghai: K'ai-ming shu-tien, 1937), pp. 57–60.

76. Wang Ch'i, *Li Ch'ang-chi ko-shih*, p. 151; Yeh Ts'ung-ch'i, *Li Ho shih-chi* (Peking, 1959), p. 274; Saitō, *Ri Ga* (Tokyo: Shūeisha, 1967), p. 303.

77. This line has also puzzled many commentators. Wang Ch'i comments: "*tung-tung*, the sound of drums; however, it does not fit with the preceeding five characters. I suspect there might be some spurious writing in the text." Suzuki Torao notes: "*Tung-tung*, the sound of a drum; before these two characters, the word 'drum' should be inserted when reading the line."

78. Wang Ch'i, *Li Ch'ang-chi Ko-shih*, p. 12; *Li Ho ko-shih-pien*, p. 15.

79. *"Ri Ga no uma no shi to To-shi"* [Li Ho's Poems on the Horses and Tu Fu's Poetry], in *Chūgoku bungaku ronshū* [Studies in Chinese Literature] dedicated to Dr. Yoshikawa Kōjirō (Tokyo: Chikuma shobō, 1958), p. 457.
80. Ibid.

Chapter Three

1. See James J. Y. Liu, *The Art of Chinese Poetry* (Chicago and London: The University of Chicago Press, 1962), pp. 91–100.
2. Wang Ssu-jen, "Preface to *Ch'ang-ku shih-chieh,*" in *San-chia p'ing-chu Li Ch'ang-chi ko-shih,* p. 28.
3. Li Tung-yang, *Lu-t'ang shih-hua* [Lu-t'ang's Comments on Poetry], *Ts'ung-shu chi-ch'eng* edition, p. 12.
4. Cf. James J. Y. Liu, *The Art of Chinese Poetry,* pp. 110–150, and Liu, *The Poetry of Li Shang-yin* (Chicago and London: The University of Chicago Press, 1969), pp. 220–48.
5. Fan Hsi-wen, *Tui-ch'uang yeh-yü* [Talks at Night with Beds Put Together], *Ts'ung-shu chi-ch'eng* edition, Vol. II, p. 15.
6. Kamio Ryūsuke, *"Yoru no shijin",* p. 14.
7. Ibid., p. 13.
8. Arai Ken, *"Ri Ga no shi—toku ni sono shikisai ni tsuite"* [On Li Ho's Poetry, Especially His Employment of Colors], *Chūgoku Bungaku-hō* [Journal of Chinese Literature], Vol. 3 (1955), p. 61.
9. Kamio Ryūsuke, *"Yoru no shijin,"* p. 15. The author mistakenly gives the total for his figures as 229, instead of 230.
10. Max Lüscher, *The Lüscher Color Test,* tr. by Ian Scott, (New York: Random House, 1969), pp. 9–19.
11. Gertrude Jobes, *Dictionary of Mythology, Folklore, and Symbols* (New York: Scarecrow Press, 1962), p. 1677.
12. Emanuel Swedenborg (1688–1772), quoted in Jobes, ibid.
13. Lüscher, *The Lüscher Color Test,* pp. 63–65, 69.
14. Richard Wilhelm, *I Ching* [The Book of Changes], tr. by Cary F. Baynes (Princeton, N. J. : Princeton University Press, 1967), pp. xlvii–lxii.
15. Lüscher, pp. 58–60.
16. Jobes, *Dictionary of Mythology,* p. 1327.
17. C. A. S. Williams, *Outlines of Chinese Symbolism and Art Motives* (Rutland, Vt. & Tokyo: Charles E. Tuttle Company, 1974), pp. 79, 189.
18. Lüscher, pp. 60–62.
19. Wang Ssu-jen, "Preface to *Ch'ang-ku shih-chieh.*" See note 2 above.
20. Buson Yosa, *Buson shū* [Works of Buson], in *Nihon koten bungaku taikei* [Japanese Classical Literature Series] (Tokyo: Iwanami shoten, 1959), Vol. 58, p. 57.
21. Yang Shen, *"Chu-hsiang"* [Bamboo Fragrance], *Sheng-yen shih-hua*

[Sheng-yen's Comments on Poetry], *Ts'ung-shu chi-ch'eng* edition, p. 192.

22. Ch'ien Chung-shu, *T'an yi lu*, p. 57.

23. T. S. Eliot, "The Metaphysical Poets," *Selected Essays* (New York, 1932), p. 249.

24. Ibid., p. 246.

25. Quoted by Wang Ch'i in *San-chia p'ing-chu Li Ch'ang-chi ko-shih*, p. 28. Ironically, the word *kuei* (ghost or demon), the epithet often used to characterize Li Ho's genius, is not included in the list of Li Ho's "favored" words (356 in all) provided by M. A. Robertson in her dissertation on Li Ho's poetic diction (pp. 78–80). A "favored" word, in Robertson's definition, is one used *more than ten times;* unfortunately, Li Ho used the word *kuei only ten times.* The statistical approach does not take into account the fact that the reader may be far more deeply impressed by such a word than one he used 147 times: *jen* (man).

26. Seto Yasuo, *"Ri Ga zatsuron,"* p. 83.

27. Wang Li-hsi, *Li Ch'ang-chi p'ing-chuan* [A Critical Biography of Li Ch'ang-chi] (Shanghai: Shen-chou kuo-kuang-she, 1930), p. 69.

28. Kao Yu-kung and Mei Tsu-lin, "Syntax, Diction, and Imagery in T'ang Poetry," *Harvard Journal of Asian Studies* Vol. 31 (1971), p. 60.

29. Cf. Liu, *Art of Chinese Poetry*, pp. 26–27.

30. Liu, *Poetry of Li Shang-yin*, pp. 228–29.

31. Wang Shih-chen, *Ch'üan T'ang shih-sho* [On T'ang Poetry], *Ts'ung-shu chi-ch'eng* edition, p. 7.

32. According to Bernhard Karlgren, *Grammata Serica Recensa* (Göteborg: Elanders Boktryckeri Aktiebolag, 1964).

33. My statistics about rhyme words are all based on "The Rhyming Categories of Li Ho" by E. G. Pullybank, in *Tsing Hua Journal of Chinese Studies*, New Series, Vol. VII, No. 1, 1968.

34. Ch'ien Chung-shu, *T'an yi lu*, p. 57.

35. In "Preface to *Li Ch'ang-chi ko-shih*," Tu Mu remarks: "Presumably as a successor of the *Li Sao* tradition, although his '*li*' does not come up to that of the *Li Sao*, his '*tz'u*' sometimes surpasses it . . . If Ho had not died and had added a little more '*li*' to his works, he could have commanded the *Li Sao* as a slave or a servant." The meaning of "*li*" here is quite ambiguous. I think it has a double meaning: one is "logic," referring to his way of thinking. Some of Li Ho's images are so wild and capricious that they are thought to be illogical. The other meaning is "reason," referring to common sense or commonly accepted ideas. Li Ho's images are often contrary to ordinary thinking; they seem unreasonable or obscure to the reader who does not understand their "inner logic."

36. Seto Yasuo, *"Ri Ga zatsuron,"* p. 83.

37. Young Shen: Shen Ch'ung of the Chin dynasty (265–419), who coined small money which was called "Young Shen's coins," here referring to elm pods.

38. Seto Yasuo, pp. 83–84.

39. I owe this interpretation to Mr. Lin Kuo-yüan, a reader of my article on this poem published in *Li Poetry Magazine*, No. 60, Taipei, April, 1974.

40. Liu Ch'en-weng, *T'ang Li Ch'ang-chi ko-shih*, pp. 12–13. For Wang Ch'i's disagreement with Liu, see *San-chia p'ing-chu ko-shih*, p. 13.

41. Liu, *The Art of Chinese Poetry*, p. 102.

42. Ibid., pp. 107–109.

43. Ch'ien Chung-shu, *T'an yi lu*, p. 68.

44. Quoted by Hu Tzu in *T'iao-hsi Yü-yin ts'ung-hua* [Collected Comments of T'iao-hsi Yü-yin], *chüan* 53, *Ts'ung-shu chi-ch'eng* edition, p. 363.

45. Hsieh Chen, *Ssu-ming shih-hua* [Ssu-ming's Comments on Poetry], *chüan* 2, *Ts'ung-shu chi-ch'eng* edition, p. 22.

46. Hung Liang-chi, *Pei-chiang shih-hua* [Pei-chiang's Comments on Poetry], *chüan* 5, *Ts' ung-shu chi-ch'eng* edition, p. 59.

47. Liu, *Art of Chinese Poetry*, pp. 102–104.

48. Ibid.

49. "Chant d'automne" [Song of Autumn] in *Les Fleurs du Mal*, Tr. William Aggeler, op. cit., p. 195: "It seems to me, lulled by these monstrous shocks,/That somewhere they're nailing a coffin in great haste./For whom?"

Chapter Four

1. See Liu, *Art of Chinese Poetry*, pp. 26–27.

2. *Ch'ing-nien chieh*, Vol. V, No. 2, quoted by Chu Tzu-ch'ing in his *Li Ho nien-p'u* [Chronological Biography of Li Ho].

3. See "Biography of Li Ho" in both *New T'ang History* and *Old T'ang History*.

4. Chu Chün-yi, *"Li Ch'ang-chi ko-shih yüan-liu chü-yü"* [The Sources and Influences of Li Ch'ang-chi's Poetry: a Study with Examples], *Tung-fang tsa-chih* [The Eastern Miscellany], New Series, Vol. 5, No. 11 (1972), pp. 57–58.

5. This is pointed out in *Yü-tung hsü-lu* [Introductory Notes of Yü-tung], quoted by Wang Ch'i, *Li Ch'ang-chi ko-shih*, p. 26.

6. Tu Fu, *Tu Kung-pu chi*, *chüan* 11, p. 106.

7. Han Yü, *Han Ch'ang-li wen-chi*, *chüan* 2, p. 6a.

8. Chou Ch'eng-chen, *Li Ho lun* [A Study of Li Ho] (Hong Kong: Wen-yi shu-wu, 1972), pp. 143–44.

9. Ibid.

10. Sung Ch'i (997–1061) is quoted as the first source for the characterization of Li Ho as a *kuei-ts'ai* and Li Po as a *hsien-ts'ai* in *Wen-hsien t'ung-k'ao* (Shanghai: The Commercial Press, 1936), *chüan* 242, p. 1917.

11. Wada Toshio, *"Ri Ga no kishi to sono keisei"* [Li Ho's *kuei* Poetry and Its Formation], *Gunma daigaku kiyō jinbun kagaku hen* [Gunma University Bulletin: Humanities] Vol 5, No. 8 (1956); 89–102.

12. Ibid., p. 91

13. *Yang-yi-chai shih-hua* [Yang-yi-chai's Comments on Poetry], Vol. V, quoted by Wada, *"Ri Ga no kishi,"* p. 94.

14. Tu Fu, *Tu Kung-pu chi, chüan* 10, p. 54.

15. *Li T'ai-po shih-chi* [Collected Poems of Li Po], *Ssu-pu pei-yao, chüan* 23, p. 26.

16. Liu Ling (221?–300?): a poet of the Chin dynasty who abandoned himself to drinking and wrote an essay extolling the virtues of wine.

17. According to *Tōdai no shihen* [Poems of the T'ang Dynasty], Hiraoka Takeo, ed. (Kyoto: Jimbunkagaku kenkyūjo, 1964).

18. Suzuki Torao, *Ri Chōkichi kashishū*, p. 3.

19. Yü Kuang-chung, "To the White Jade Palace: A Critical Study of Li Ho," *Tamkang Journal*, No. 7 (1968), p. 221.

20. David Ch'en, "Li Ho and Keats: Poverty, Illness, Frustration, and a Poetic Career," *Tsing Hua Journal of Chinese Studies*, New Series, Vol. V, No. 1 (1965), p. 81.

21. A. C. Graham, *Poems of the Late T'ang* (Baltimore: Penguin Books, 1968), p. 91.

22. Wang Chin-p'ing (tr.), *"Li Ho shih chung te ch'ao hsien-shih yi-hsiang"* [Surrealistic Images in Li Ho's Poetry], *Yu-shih wen-yi*, No. 233 (1973), p. 9. The original article was written by William C. Golightly, but the source was not indicated.

23. Yü Kuang-chung, *"To the White Jade Palace,"* p. 221.

24. Ibid.

25. Su Hsüeh-lin, *T'ang-shih kai-lun* [An introduction to T'ang Poetry], (Taipei: The Commercial Press, 1958), p. 146.

26. Lin Keng, *Chung-kuo wen-hsüeh-shih* [A History of Chinese Literature] (Amoy: Amoy University, 1947), p. 211.

27. Yü Kuang-chung, "To the White Jade Palace," p. 222.

Finding-List of Titles of Li Ho's Poems Mentioned in the Text

Abbreviations of Editions

KSP *Li Ho ko-shih-pien* (National Central Library edition)
LCCKS *Li Ch'ang-chi ko-shih* (commentary by Wang Ch'i)
PLH *The Poems of Li Ho* (translated by J. D. Frodsham)

Numbers in boldface indicate the poems discussed in the text.

KSP	LCCKS	PLH	Titles	Page in Text
17	35–36	10–11	Song: Li P'ing on the *K'ung-hou* Harp	**76–77,** 100, 110
17–18	36	12	Song: Lingering Threads	**104,** 109
18	36–37	13	Song: Returning from Kuei-chi	31, 88, 99, 126
19	37	14	Sent to Ch'üan Ch'ü and Yang Ching-chih While Leaving the City	29, 33
19	37–38	15	Shown to My Younger Brother	99
19–20	38	16	Bamboo	99
20–21	39–40	18	Upon Assuming My Post as Supervisor of Ceremonies, I Recall My Ch'ang-ku Mountain Dwelling	26
21	40	19	Seventh Night	
21–22	40	20	Passing by Hua-ch'ing Palace	125
23–24	42	23–24	Expressing Feelings (Two Poems)	100, 115
24	42–43	24–25	Written After a Poem by Liu Yün	100
24–25	43–44	25	Song: The Sword of the Collator in the Spring Office	95, 107, 116

149

Selected Bibliography

According to Tu Mu's *Preface* (A.D. 831), Li Ho on his deathbed gave his poems, 233 in all divided into four sections, to his friend Shen Tzu-wen. This is the earliest record of Li Ho's poems. Later bibliographical notices are different: *Hsin T'ang-shu yi-wen-chih* (*chüan* 60): *Li Ho chi*, 5 *chüan*; *Sung-shih yi-wen-chih* (*chüan* 208): *Li Ho chi*, I *chüan*, and *wai-chi*, I *ch-üan*; *Wen-hsien t'ung-k'ao* (*chüan* 242): *Li Ch'ang-chi chi*, 4 *chüan*. (The bibliographical notice in *Ssu-k'u chüan-shu tsung-mu t'i-yao*, which is in error, was followed by Suzuki, Saitō, Frodsham, and Yeh Ts'ung-ch'i.)

According to T'ien Pei-hu, the earliest edition of Li Ho's works he had seen is the Pien edition, dated 1067, the fourth year of the *Chih-p'ing* period of Northern Sung. *Li Ch'ang-chi ko-shih* annotated by Wu Cheng-tzu and Liu Ch'en-weng is generally considered to be the earliest commentated edition; it was published in 1337. Wu consulted five Sung editions extant at the time: the Capital edition (219 poems), the Shu edition (219 poems), the Kuei-chi edition (219 poems), the Hsüan-ch'eng edition (242 poems), and the Pao family edition (242 poems). Wu considered the Pao family edition to be superior to the others and used it as the basis for his commentary. He deleted one poem as a repetition and included 219 poems in four *chüan* as *pen-chi* (main collection) and twenty-two poems in one *chüan* as *wai-chi* (extra collection), totalling 241 poems. Although Li Ho's original works, as Tu Mu indicated, contained 233 poems arranged, probably by the poet himself, in four sections, after Sung·times most editions had 219 poems in the *pen-chi* and various numbers of poems in the *wai-chi*. The reasons for these discrepancies in numbers and how the *wai-chi* came into existence are not clear.

154

PRIMARY SOURCES

A. Editions of Li Ho's works without commentaries:

1. *Li Ho ko-shih-pien*, 4 *chüan, chi-wai-shih*, 1 *chüan*. The Hsüan-ch'eng edition of Northern Sung, reprinted in facsimile by Sung-fen-shih (1918) and by National Central Library (Taipei, 1971) with a valuable introduction authenticating its date and arguing its superiority.

2. *Li Ch'ang-chi wen-chi*, 4 *chüan*. Photolithographic reprint of the Shu edition of Northern Sung, included in *Hsü ku-yi ts'ung-shu*. Shanghai: Han-fen-lou, 1922; photoreprinted by Hsüeh-sheng shu-chü (Taipei, 1967). The *wai-chi* in the Hsüeh-sheng shu-chü edition is from the *Chin-nang-chi*; see below no. 5.

3. *Li Ho ko-shih-pien*, 4 *chüan, chi-wai-shih*, 1 *chüan*. Photolithographic reprint of the Northern Sung edition included in *Mi-yün-lou ying Sung-pen ch'i-chung*, compiled by Chiang Ju-tsao in the early republican era.

4. *Ko-shih-pien*, 4 *chüan*. The so-called Chin edition, included in *T'ieh-ch'in-t'ung-chien-lou ts'ung-shu*, compiled by Chü Ch'i-chia of the republican era, and in *Ssu-pu ts'ung-k'an (chi-pu)*. Shanghai: The Commercial Press, 1919, 1929, 1936. According to Professor Cheng Ch'ien and the late Wang Kuo-wei, the original edition was published in 1256, twenty-two years after the Chin dynasty was conquered by the Mongolians; therefore, it should rightfully be called the Mongolian edition.

5. *Chin-nang-chi*, 4 *chüan, wai-chi*, 1 *chüan*. Photolithographic reprint of the Yüan edition (1177), included in *Hsiu-shui Chin-shih mei-hua ts'ao-t'ang ying-yin shan-pen chih-erh* (1923). Microfilmed by the National Central Library, Taipei, 1973.

B. Editions with commentaries (given in chronological order)

1. [Yüan]. WU CHENG-TZU and LIU CH'EN-WENG. *Li Ch'ang-chi ko-shih*, 4 *chüan, wai-chi*, 1 *chüan*. Published by Fu-ku-t'ang in 1337, included in *Ssu-k'u ch'üan-shu (chi-pu, pieh-chi-lei)*, reprinted by Shōheizaka Gakumonjo, Edo (Kyoto), 1819; by Kyoto University Library, 1952; and by the Commercial Press (Taipei, 1973) in *Ssu-k'u ch'üan-shu chen-pen (ssu-chi*, No. 225). Microfilmed by the National Central Library, Taipei, 1975. Earliest commentary on Li Ho's works based on the Pao family edition; many later commentators use it as a source.

2. [Ming] HSÜ WEI and TUNG MAO-TS'E. *T'ang Li Ch'ang-chi shi-chi*, 5 *chüan (pen-chi*, 4 *chüan, wai-chi*, 1 *chüan, shou*, 1 *chüan)*. Originally two separate works both entitled *Ch'ang-ku shih-chu*, reprinted in *Tung-shih ts'ung-shu*, compiled and published by Tung Chin-chien, 1906.

3. TSENG YI. *Ch'ang-ku chi*, 4 *chüan*. Published in the Wan-li period

(1573–1619) of Ming, included in *Kuo-hsüeh chi-pen ts'ung-shu* (Basic collections of Chinese classics). Shanghai: The Commercial Press, 1941. Also included in *Li Ho shih-chu* (Commentaries of Li Ho's poems). Taipei: Shih-chieh shu-chü, 1953.

4. YÜ KUANG. *Ch'ang-ku shih-chu*. A Ming edition mentioned by Wang Ch'i (See below no. 10) who saw its preface and some notes quoted from it written on the margins of an edition of Li Ho's works with commentary by Hsü Wei and Tung Mao-ts'e (See above no. 2). No other scholars' note attests to its present existence.

5. YAO CH'ÜAN and CH'IU HSIANG-SUI. *Li Ch'ang-chi Ch'ang-ku chi chü-chieh ting-pen*, 4 *chüan*. Date presumed to be 1654. In addition to Yao's commentary, also includes six scholars' notes and comments by seven others.

6. [Ch'ing] HUANG T'AO-AN and LI ERH-CH'IAO. *Li Ch'ang-chi chi*, 4 *chüan*, *wai-chi*, 1 *chüan*. Huang's comments dated 1731; Li's, 1773. Reprinted by Yeh Yen-lan (the Yang-ch'eng editions), 1892, and by Sao-yeh shan-fang, 1909.

7. YAO WEN-HSIEH. *Ch'ang-ku chi*, 4 *chüan*, *chi-wai-shih*, 1 *chüan*. Commentator's foreword dated 1657, included in *Lung-min ts'ung-shu* compiled by Kuang Ts'ung-hsieh. Also included in *San-chia p'ing-chu Li Ch'ang-chi ko-shih* (Li Ho's poems annotated and commented by three scholars). Peking: Chung-hua shu-chü, 1959, and in *Li Ho shih-chu* (See above no. 3). Effort on the part of the commentator to relate Li Ho's lines to historical events or incidents in the life of the poet. In many cases, farfetched and misleading.

8. FANG FU-NAN. *Li Ch'ang-chi shih-chi*, 4 *chüan*. Preface dated 1751, included in *San-chia p'ing-chu Li Ch'ang-chi ko'shih* and *Li Ho shih-chu*.

9. SHIH JUNG. *Li Ch'ang-chi ko-shih pu-chu*, 18 *chüan*, with an old edition, 5 *chüan*, chronology, 1 *chüan*, appendix, 1 *chüan*, shou, 1 *chüan*. Hand-copied manuscripts (21 *ts'e*), included in the Exhibition of Chekiang Cultural Heritage, July-December, 1936. Highly respected but unavailable.

10. WANG CH'I. *Li Ch'ang-chi ko-shih*, 4 *chüan*, wai-chi 1 *chüan*, shou, 1 *chüan*. Published by Pao-hu-lou in 1760, reprinted in *Ssu-pu pei-yao* (Essentials of the four libraries), *San-chia p'ing-chu Li Ch'ang-chi ko-shih* and *Li Ho shih-chu*. Comprehensive "standard" commentary, synthesis of various scholars' opinions, broadly elucidating allusions.

11. CH'EN PEN-LI. *Hsieh-lü kou-yüan*, 5 *chüan* (pen-chi, 4 *chüan* wai-chi, 1 *chüan*). The Yi-lu-hsüan edition, preface dated 1808, included in *Chiang-tu Ch'en-shih ts'ung-shu*. Reprinted in facsimile by the Chinese University of Hong Kong in 1973. Valuable, provides several original interpretations.

12. WU JU-LUN. *Li Ch'ang-chi shih p'ing-chu*, 4 *chüan*, *wai-chi*, 1 *chüan*.

Published in 1922, with an afterword written by Wu K'an-sheng, the commentator's son.
13. YEH TS'UNG-CH'I. *Li Ho shih-chi.* Peking: Jen-min wen-hsüeh ch'u-pan-she, 1959. The only edition in modern Chinese, includes notes, an interpretation of each poem, and seeks to rectify errors by previous scholars. Most useful for modern readers.
14. CH'EN HUNG-CHIH. *Li Ch'ang-chi ko-shih chiao-shih.* Taipei: Chia-hsin shui-ni kung-ssu wen-hua chi-chin-hui, 1969. Comprehensive collection of scholarly notes and comments with rectification of errors in various editions.

SECONDARY SOURCES

Works in Chinese
1. Concordance
AI, WEN-PO (Robert L. Irick). *Li Ho shih yin-te* (A Concordance to the Poems of Li Ho). Taipei: Chinese Materials and Research Aids Service Center, 1969. Based on *Li Ch'ang-chi ko-shih* commented by Wang Ch'i. Indispensable for Li Ho scholars.
2. Chronology
CHU, TZU-CH'ING. *Li Ho nien-p'u* (Chronological Biography of Li Ho), *Ch'ing-hua hsüeh-pao (Tsing Hua Journal of Chinese Studies),* Vol. X, No. 4 (1935), pp. 46–85. Included in *Wen-shih lun-chu* (Critical Works on Literature and History). Hong Kong: T'ai-p'ing shu-chü, 1962, pp. 46–87. Most reliable, based on sound scholarship.
3. Critical studies (given in chronological order)
SU, HSÜEH-LIN. "*Li Ho te shih-ko*" (On Li Ho's Poetry), 1926. Included in *Hsüeh-lin tzu-hsüen-chi* (Selected Works of Su Hsüeh-lin). Taipei: Hsin-lu shu-chü, 1954, pp. 95–105. One of the earliest articles.
WANG, LI-HSI. *Li Ch'ang-chi p'ing-chuan* (Critical Biography of Li Ch'ang-chi). Shanghai: Shen-chou kuo-kuang-she, 1930. A unique work on Li Ho's life, character and poetry from a Marxist viewpoint.
HO, YANG-LING. *Li Ch'ang-chi ko-shi* (The Poems of Li Ch'ang-chi). Shanghai: Kuang-hua shu-chü, 1933. Reprinted by Hua-shih ch'u-pan-she, Taipei, 1975. Early work looking into some interesting aspects of the poet and his poetry.
CHOU, LANG-FENG. *Shih-jen Li Ho* (The Poet Li Ho). Shanghai: The Commercial Press, 1936. Pioneer work, balanced coverage of the poet's life, style, character, and critic's opinions.
CH'IEN, CHUNG-SHU. *T'an yi lu* (Comments on Art). Shanghai: K'ai-ming shu-chü, 1937, pp. 58–74. Provides insights into Li Ho's poetic characteristics.
CHOU, CH'ENG-CHEN. *Li Ho lun* (Studies of Li Ho). Hong Kong: Wen-yi shu-wu, 1972. "Intrinsic" study of Li Ho's poems with some illumining interpretations and sensible analysis.

Works in Japanese
1. Translations (given in chronological order)
URUSHIYAMA, MATASHIRŌ. *Yaku-chū Ri Chōkichi shishū* (A Translation
with Notes of the Collected Poems of Li Ch'ang-chi). Tokyo: Tōmei
shoyin, 1933. Pioneer work in Japanese, not always accurate in transla-
tion.
ARAI, KEN. *Ri Ga* [Li Ho], *(Chūgoku shijin senshū,* 14) (Selected Works of
Chinese Poets). Tokyo: Iwanami shoten, 1959. Seventy-six poems
translated with notes and an enlightening introduction.
SUZUKI, TORAO. *Ri Chōkichi kashishū* (The Poems of Li Ch'ang-chi),
(Iwanami bunko), 2 vols. Tokyo: Iwanami shoten, 1961. Provides many
original interpretations, but not always supportable.
SAITŌ, SHŌ. *Ri Ga* (Li Ho), *(Kanshi taikei* 13) (Chinese Poets Series).
Tokyo: Shūeisha, 1967. Synthesis of previous scholarly opinions with a
critical attitude.
2. Studies
HARADA, KENYŪ. *"Ri Chōkichi o mequtte"* (Studies of Li Ch'ang-chi). Eight
articles under this general title published in *Hōkō* (Direction), Nos.
1–9. Kyoto: Hōkō-sha, March, 1953–August, 1960.
————. *"Ri Ga shōki"* (Notes of Studies of Li Ho). Seven articles under this
general title published in *Jinbun ronsō* (Studies of Humanities), Nos. 7,
8, 14–18. Kyōto: Kyōto Woman University Humanities Society,
November, 1962–June, 1970, and two articles published in *Hōkō* (Nos.
10 and 13), July, 1964 and March, 1967. Wholehearted devotion to
study of Li Ho; broad historical investigation and useful tangential
materials.
————. *Ri Ga kenkyū* (Li Ho Studies). A private journal published irregu-
larly since January, 1971, Kyoto. Headquarters for Japanese sources
related to Li Ho.
KUSAMORI, SHIN'ICHI. *"Suishō no kyaku-Ri Chōkichi den"* (The Pinions-
Drooping Traveler—Biography of Li Ch'ang-chi). Part I (14 chapters)
and part II (46 chapters) serialized in *Gendai-shi techō* (Notebook of
Modern Poetry) since 1965, Tokyo. Energetic and devoted biography,
broadly includes information on the times and other figures contemporary with Li Ho; hypothesizes boldly and investigates scrupulously.

Works in English
1. English translations (given in chronological order)
GILES, HERBERT A. *A History of Chinese Literature,* p. 175. London:
D. Appleton and Company, 1901. Includes one of Li Ho's poems, e.g.
"Shao-nien lo" ("Joy of Youth"), a supplement added by Wang Ch'i.
The earliest English translation of Li Ho's poems.
PAYNE, ROBERT. *The White Pony.* New York: John Day Company, 1947.

Pp. 293–318 include thirty of Li Ho's poems translated by Ho Chih-yüan.

CH'EN, JEROME and BULLOCK, MICHAEL. *Poems of Solitude*. London New York Toronto: Abelard-Schuman, 1960. Pp. 81–95 include twelve of Li Ho's poems.

YANG HSIEN-YI and GLADYS YANG. "Selections from the Classics." *Chinese Literature*, No. 12 (1963). Pp. 65–73 contain eleven of Li Ho's poems.

GRAHAM, A. C. *Poems of the Late T'ang*. Baltimore: Penguin books, 1965. Pp. 89–119 contain twenty-two of Li Ho's poems.

FRODSHAM, J. D. *The Poems of Li Ho* (791–817). Oxford: Clarendon Press, 1970. First complete English translation with notes; painstaking accomplishment mainly based on Japanese commentaries.

WU-CHI LIU and IRVING YUCHENG LO. *Sunflower Splendor*. New York: Anchor Press / Doubleday, 1975. Pp. 288–236 contain eleven of Li Ho's poems translated by Maureen Robertson, Michael Fish, and Irving Y. Lo.

ANONYMOUS, "Writings by Legalists." *Chinese Literature*, No. 2 (1976). Pp. 87–93 contain five of Li Ho's poems.

2. Critical Studies and Articles

CH'EN, DAVID YING. "Li Ho and Keats: A Comparative Study of Two Poets." Unpublished doctoral dissertation, Indiana University, Bloomington, 1962.

_____. "Li Ho and Keats: Poverty, Illness, Frustration and a Poetic Career." *Tsing Hua Journal of Chinese Studies*. New Series V, No. 1 (1965), pp. 67–84.

CH'EN, YI-HSIN. "Li Ho, a poetic Genius." *Chinese Literature*, No. 12 (1963), pp. 74–80.

CHUNG WEN. "Legalist Ideas in Li Ho's Poetry." *Chinese Literature*, No. 2 (1976), pp. 94–100. This and several articles in Chinese claiming Li Ho "a legalist poet" indicate the new official attitude adopted by Communist Chinese scholars.

FISH, MICHAEL B. "Mythological Themes in the Poetry of Li Ho (791–817)." Unpublished doctoral dissertation, Indiana University, Bloomington, 1973.

_____. "The Striving of a Young Man at Twenty: Li Ho's Poem 'Wildly Singing.' " Pp. 59–70 in *Critical Essays on Chinese Literature*, William H. Nienhauser, Jr., ed. Hong Kong: The Chinese University of Hong Kong, 1976.

GRAHAM, A. C. "A New Translation of a Chinese Poet, Li Ho." *Bulletin of the School of Oriental and African Studies*, Vol. 34 (1971), pp. 560–70.

KUDŌ, NAOTARŌ. *The Life and Thoughts of Li Ho*. Tokyo: Waseda University Press, 1969. A critical biography with extensive historical and literary background of the times.

PULLEYBLANK, E. G. "The Rhyming Categories of Li Ho (791–817)." *Tsing*

Hua Journal of Chinese Studies, New Series VII, No. 1 (1968), pp. 1–22.

ROBERTSON, MAUREEN A. "Poetic Diction in the Works of Li Ho (891–917) [*sic.*]." Unpublished doctoral dissertation, University of Washington, Seattle, 1970.

SCHAFER, E. H. "The Goddess Epiphanies of Li Ho." Pp. 104–114 in *The Divine Woman: The Dragon Ladies and Rain Maidens in T'ang Literature*. Berkeley, Los Angeles & London: University of California Press, 1973.

SOUTH, MARGARET TUDOR. "Li Ho—A Scholar-official of the Yüan-ho Period (806–821)." *Journal of the Oriental Society of Australia*, Vol. II, No. 2 (1964), pp. 64–81.

――――. "Li Ho and the New *Yüeh-fu* Movement." *Journal of the Oriental Society of Australia*, Vol. IV, No. 2 (1966), pp. 49–61.

――――. *Li Ho: a Scholar-official of the Yüan-ho Period (806–821)*. Adelaide: Libraries Board of South Australia, 1967. Historical study of the life and times of the poet, provides much useful and well-grounded information.

SUTHERLAND, JOAN. "Li Ho and the Lankavatara Sutra." *Journal of Asian Culture*, Vol. II, No. 1 (Spring 1978), pp. 69–102. The Graduate Students in Asian Studies at UCLA.

TU, KUO-CH'ING. "The Poetry of Li Ho: A Critical Study." Unpublished doctoral dissertation, Stanford University, Stanford, 1974.

WELLS, H. W. "Li Ho's Creative Genius." *Tamkang Review*, Vol. VI, No. 1 (April 1975), pp. 77–97.

YÜ, KWANG-CHUNG. "To the White Jade Palace: A Critical Study of Li Ho (791–817)." *Tamkang Journal*, No. 7 (November, 1968), pp. 193–224.

Index